From the *E.F.S.* equine series

Explaining

LAMINITIS
and its
PREVENTION

ROBERT A. EUSTACE
BVSc Cert E.O. Cert E.P. MRCVS

Director of the
LAMINITIS CLINIC, UNIVERSITY OF BRISTOL.

Foreword by Susan McBane

Copyright 1996 by Robert A. Eustace
The Laminitis Clinic, Mead House Farm & Stud, Dauntsey,
Chippenham, Wiltshire SN15 4JA. Telephone: 01249 890784.

First published 1992.
Reprinted 1996.

British Library Cataloguing in Publication Data.

Eustace, Robert A.
  Explaining Laminitis and its Prevention
  I. Title II. Series
  636.1

Printed and bound in Great Britain at J. W. Arrowsmith Ltd, Bristol.

Cover design Ken Ashman and Robert Eustace.

UK Distributor
Equi Life Supply, Mead House Farm, Dauntsey, Chippenham,
Wiltshire SN15 4JA.
Telephone: 01249 890784.

ISBN 0-9518974-0-3

FOREWORD

My first experience of a pony with laminitis occurred many years ago when my best friend's pony, Blighty, went down, literally, with a very bad attack of it. Despite being so long ago, I can remember the distress we all felt at his obvious suffering, the worry of the family, the very frequent visits of the vet. and the sheer difficulty of managing Blighty and treating him as advised.

He was down, groaning and sweating with pain. The vet. got him to his feet, gave him various injections we did not understand, including painkillers so that he could bear to stand and walk around 'to get his circulation going again'. He was put on a starvation diet and, being very fond of his food, this alone caused him and the family sufficient distress seeing him hungry and obviously uncomfortable as well as in pain from the laminitis. On top of everything he, not surprisingly with hindsight, got colic as well! Blighty was nursed for several weeks but in the end was put down.

All this was a long time ago, but it seems that the usual treatment for laminitis runs along rather similar lines to that which Blighty received. Now, however, thanks to pioneering research and practice in the United States and at the Laminitis Clinic at Bristol University, we know better. The disease is still a killer and excruciatingly painful for the animal concerned, but we now know much more about it, about what happens during laminitis and about how to prevent and treat it.

This book is the only one presently available which passes on to the 'ordinary' horse and pony owner, with perhaps little scientific knowledge and who has been brought up along very traditional lines as far as horse management is concerned, the state-of-the-art knowledge which can now save the lives of affected animals and probably prevent them developing laminitis in the first place.

We now know it is quite wrong to force-walk laminitic animals, to inject them with corticosteroids and to put them on 'starvation' diets, although these practices are still often regarded as standard remedies.

Laminitic animals need very specific management, veterinary treatment and nutrition without 'starvation'. This book explains fully, in easily-understood terms, our present knowledge of the disease and how to prevent it, and, therefore, how to save your horse or pony's life. It is written by a world authority on the disease who has saved the lives of very many animals who would otherwise have been put down, in many cases restoring the animals concerned to working lives.

You will learn how to recognise laminitis quickly with simple daily checks, you will come to understand the vital importance of prompt treatment of the correct kind and how essential correct management and nutrition (detailed in this book) are to both prevention of and recovery from laminitis. You will no longer have to cope with a chronically laminitic animal because the fact is that if your horse or pony has had laminitis once there is almost certainly no need for him to get it again. If you follow the advice in this book, its recurrence is not inevitable.

Probably most important of all, you will learn how to recognise it if it does occur and how to prevent it in the first place. You may be surprised at some of the advice you read as it is contrary to what has been, and still is, widely believed and taught about laminitis. But you can rely completely on the advice in these pages as being the most up-to-date and reliable so far available. If everyone follows this advice laminitis will become a rare disease.

Susan McBane

January 1992

CONTENTS

LIST OF FIGURES

Figure 13.
Diagrammatic representation of the normal split foot shown in Figure 12.

Figure 14.
Split foot of a case of acute founder.

Figure 15.
Diagrammatic representation of the acute founder foot in Figure 14.

Figure 16.
High powered view of the coronary papillae in the midline from a case of acute founder.

Figure 17.
How to feel for the depression at the coronary band indicative of acute founder.

Figure 18.
High powered view of the coronary papillae from a sinker case.

Figure 19.
A foot showing the classical changes of chronic founder.

Figure 20.
Solar view of foot prior to taking an X-ray.

Figure 21.
Front view of foot prepared for taking an X-ray.

Figure 22.
Lateral X-ray of a normal foot showing the markers.

Figure 23.
Fitting a frog support made of a part roll of bandage.

Figure 24.
Frog support in place and marked to show relative weight bearing.

Figure 25.
An X-ray of an early case of acute founder.

Figure 26.
A good example of an all steel non-adjustable heart bar shoe correctly fitted.

Figure 27.
An all steel adjustable heart bar shoe.

Figure 28.
The plastic and steel glue-on adjustable heart bar shoe (Eustace shoe) developed at the Laminitis Clinic.

Figure 29.
X-ray of a foot of a sinker.

Figure 30.
The first part of a dorsal wall resection performed on a case at the old founder stage.

Figure 31.
X-ray of a front foot of an Arab mare at the old founder stage, 7 weeks after the acute founder.

Figure 32.
Another X-ray at the old founder stage, this time with a much larger gas pocket.

Figure 33.
Front foot at the old founder stage following removal of the detached hoof wall.

Figure 34.
The same foot as in Figure 33 five months later.

Figure 35.
An X-ray of the right fore foot of the pony in Figure 36 at the old founder stage.

Figure 36.
Stance of a pony with deep digital flexor contracture of the forelimbs following quadrilateral founder.

Figure 37.
X-ray of the same foot as in Figure 35 six days later.

Figure 38.
The site for cutting the deep flexor tendon in the mid cannon region.

Figure 39.
The same pony as in Figure 36 two months later.

Figure 40.
A chronic founder Type 1 foot.

Figure 41.
Same foot as in previous Figure 10 minutes later following correct foot dressing.

Figure 42.
An old Sheltand pony's foot, an example of chronic founder Type 1.

Figure 43.
X-ray of the foot in Figure 42.

Figure 44.
X-ray of chronic founder Type 2 foot.

Figure 45.
Split foot of a chronic founder Type 2 case.

Figure 46.
Close up view of the coronary groove area in Figure 45.

Figure 47.
The site of the pituitary tumour.

Figure 48.
A typical example of the changes in hair coat of a pituitary tumour case.

Figure 49.
Not so typical of a pituitary tumour on first inspection.

Figure 50.
No wonder Tommy got laminitis!

Figure 51.
Tommy after treatment.

Figure 52.
Diagram showing the angles S, U and T.

Figure 53.
To illustrate how meaningless consideration of one angle is.

Figure 54.
Diagram showing the measurement of distances WT and D.

Figure 55.
Graph indicating the probability of an acute founder or sinker case recovering for a given founder distance D.

Figure 56.
A severe case of solar prolapse in a cob stallion.

Figure 57.
The same foot as shown in Figure 56 six months later.

To TATTY

A sweet brave mare who taught me so much

INTRODUCTION.

L aminitis is one of the most common causes of lameness and disability affecting British horses and ponies. There are some disease conditions which predispose the animal to laminitis, however most of the cases are man-made due to bad husbandry practices. Knowledge of both the disease mechanism itself and of the best treatments available has increased greatly over the last 20 years. Unfortunately, this does not mean that this information is always used for the benefit of the animals. Out of date treatment and management procedures are still being prescribed and unproven quackery is overtly advertised to the horse owning public. Some of these treatments actually worsen the condition and hurt the animal.

Before we can hope to prevent or treat laminitis an understanding is needed of how the horse's foot is constructed and how it functions. I will describe the abnormal changes which occur in the foot during laminitis in the following chapters. This will explain the difference between laminitis, founder and sinkers. Chapters on causes, treatments, prevention, feeding and prognosis follow.

Robert A Eustace MRCVS.

THE LAMINITIS CLINIC,
UNIVERSITY OF BRISTOL,
LANGFORD HOUSE,
LANGFORD.
BRISTOL.
BS18 7DU.

Chapter 1

THE

NORMAL FOOT

The pedal bone is crescent shaped, (Fig. 1), the outer surface is covered by a soft tissue called corium (Fig. 2). Corium is the same as the dermis or quick of your finger. Covering and nourished by the corium is the epidermis, the same as your skin or nails. In the horse's foot the corium is given the name of the epidermal or horny structure it supports. Thus there is perioplic corium, coronary corium, laminar corium, solar corium (sensitive sole) and frog corium (sensitive frog). At this stage it is helpful to get used to some of the terminology which has been used

Figure 1. Outer surface of the pedal bone, note how many holes or foraminae are present. In life, these contain arteries coming outwards from the terminal arch. The arteries nourish the laminar corium around the outside of the pedal bone (see Fig. 2). There are no foraminae on the underside of the pedal bone (other than at the 'wings').

Figure 2. These are the dermal laminae which cover the pedal bone. Each dermal lamina slots in between two epidermal laminae (see Fig. 3).

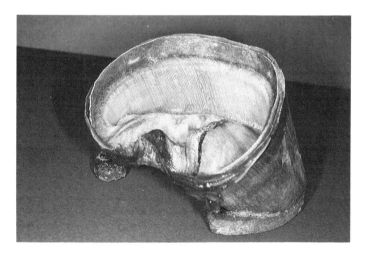

Figure 3. Covering the dermal laminae are the epidermal laminae and other horny structures which make up the hoof capsule. Above the epidermal laminae is the coronary groove (darker coloured) which contains the coronary corium.

by other authors. Laminae are sometimes called lamellae.

Corium = Dermis = Quick = Sensitive.
Dermal laminae = Soft tissue laminae = Sensitive laminae = Laminar corium.
Epidermal laminae = Horny laminae = Insensitive laminae.

The whole weight of the horse is transmitted down the bones in the legs to the pedal bone at the bottom. The pedal bone, and thus the weight of the horse, is suspended inside the horny hoof capsule by the attachment between the dermal laminae and the epidermal laminae which grow from them. There are about 600 laminae, the dermal and epidermal laminae interlock like slotting the fingers of your hands together. As the main function of the laminae is attachment of the pedal bone to the inside of the hoof capsule, it is not surprising that the surface area of the laminar corium is considerable (Figs. 3 & 4). To increase still further the area of

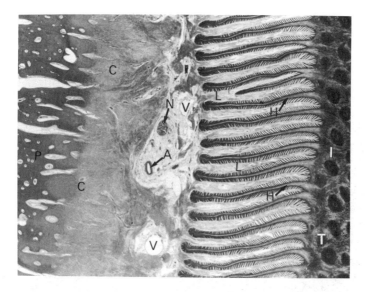

Figure 4. This is a transverse sectional view through the hoof wall as seen through the microscope. The pedal bone (P) is on the left and the outside of the hoof is on the right. The pedal bone is covered by the connective tissue (C) of the periosteum which contains arteries (A), veins (V) and nerves (N) and merges with the dermal laminae (L). The two sets of laminae, dermal (L) and epidermal (H) slot together like interlocking fingers. The tubular horn (T) from the coronary papillae and the intertubular horn (I) from the pits between the papillae are clearly visible making up the bulk of the hoof wall. (Photo courtesy of Dr Susan Kempson).

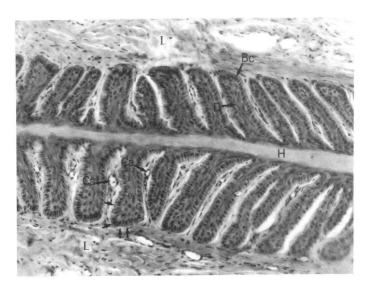

Figure 5. A higher magnification view of the interlocking dermal (L) and epidermal laminae (H). Small blood vessels (Ca) are seen within the dermal laminae. A thin lining membrane [the basement membrane] (arrowed) supports basal cells (Bc) which produce the horny epidermal laminae (H). The basal cells divide to produce daughter cells (D) which undergo keratinisation (become horny) to become the epidermal laminae (H) which can be seen in Figure 3. (Photo courtesy of Dr Susan Kempson).

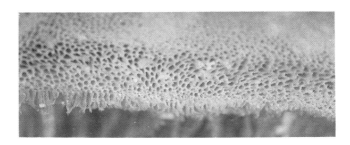

Figure 6. Close up view of the coronary groove; the inside of the hoof capsule is at the bottom of the figure. Each hole contains one coronary papilla which is responsible for the growth of one horn tubule. At the inside edge of the coronary groove the arrangement of holes changes into sheet-like laminae at the top of the laminar corium.

Figure 7. This figure shows the tissue around the coronary groove in the midline of the foot. A normal foot has been split down the midline, you are looking at the cut surface. Note the coronary papillae in longitudinal section (between the arrowheads). Their direction, pointing down to the ground at the toe and parallel to the front surface of the pedal bone, is normal. The softer perioplic horn (open arrow) is produced above the horn from the coronary corium and covers the latter for about the top inch of the wall.

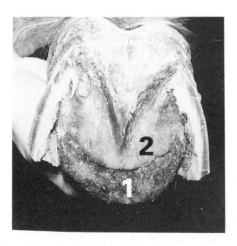

Figure 8. The sole and frog have been shed (and most of the hoof wall removed) from this pony which suffered an attack of acute founder. The figure shows how the sole and frog coria merge together, and as in this case new frog and sole horn has been produced to protect the sensitive tissues. The semi-circular outlines of the front of the pedal bone (1) and of the digital cushion (2) are as indicated. This pony made a full recovery.

attachment, there are tiny surface corrugations covering the laminae (Fig. 5).

Just as the laminar corium is specialised for attachment, so the coronary corium, which merges with the top of the laminar corium, is designed for the production of the bulk of the hoof wall. The coronary corium, instead of having leaf-like laminae over its surface, has thousands of tiny finger-like projections or papillae (Fig. 6). Each coronary papilla is responsible for the production of one horn tubule which grows down to the ground. The tubular horn is separated by inter-tubular horn which grows from the pits between the coronary papillae. The bulk of the hoof wall, produced by the coronary corium, is designed for the protection of the internal structures, abrasion resistance and shock absorption (Figs. 4 & 7).

Above the coronary corium, between it and the skin, is a narrow rim of perioplic corium. This produces a thin layer of softer tubular horn which grows over the juvenile coronary horn and offers a little protection against drying and abrasion (Fig. 7). Perioplic horn rarely extends more than about an inch down the hoof wall. Beyond this limit it is worn away by abrasion on grass or bedding.

The solar corium is attached to the bottom of the pedal bone in the front of the foot and to the under surface of the digital cushion in the back of the foot (Fig. 8). The solar corium is arranged into papillae similar to the coronary corium and thus gives rise to tubular and inter-tubular horn. Frog corium is on the underside of the digital cushion and also is formed into papillae. The horn of the frog tends to be softer than that of the sole.

From this it can be seen that two hard structures, the horny hoof capsule and the pedal bone are held together by a soft layer, the interlocking dermal and epidermal laminae. This is the only means of support for the pedal bone within the hoof; the sole and lateral cartilages play no part in keeping the pedal bone suspended within the hoof. This arrangement obviously works well most of the time, until something goes wrong with the soft layer in the middle of the sandwich!

The blood supply

The blood supply to the foot is via the paired digital arteries, one on either side of the leg. These run down the back of the leg between the suspensory ligament and the deep digital flexor tendon and emerge around the back and sides of the fetlock joint, this is the easiest place to feel for their pulsation (Fig. 9.). From there they run down the back of the pastern, giving off branches to the coronary corium all the way round the foot, and a smallish area of laminae at the back of the foot around the heels (Fig. 10). The digital arteries then pass down inside the collateral cartilages, which sit on top of the 'wings' of the pedal bone, and enter two holes on the undersurface of the pedal bone very close to the attachment of the deep digital flexor tendon. Once inside the bone they join up forming a semicircular artery known as the terminal arch. This terminal arch gives off about nine branches which go through the pedal bone and exit around the bottom rim to form another semi-circular artery, the circumflex artery of the pedal bone. This circumflex artery is outside the pedal bone and sits in a narrow space between the bottom rim of the pedal bone and the inside of the horny sole. In addition, the

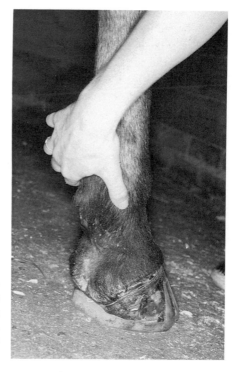

Figure 9. Where to feel for the pulsation of the digital arteries as they pass over the proximal sesamoids, an increase in the 'strength' of the pulsation indicates either an inflammatory condition in the foot or laminitis.

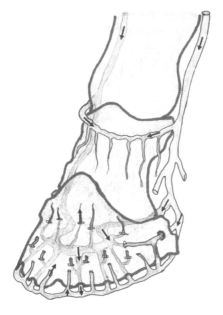

Figure 10. This diagram shows the essential features of the arterial blood supply to the foot. There are direct branches to the heels and the coronary band. The direction of blood flow is shown by the arrows.

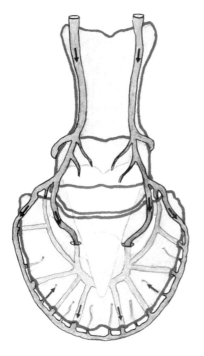

Figure 11. Diagram of the arterial supply to the foot as seen from underneath; the direction of blood flow is shown by the arrows. The large triangle represents the limits of the frog; if pressure is applied by means of a shoe which extends over the collateral frog sulci severe damage can be done to the arteries beneath. The white central area shows the position of the attachment of the deep digital flexor tendon to the underside of the pedal bone.

terminal arch gives off a few smaller branches which exit on the front surface of the pedal bone about half way up. When looked at from the front (Fig. 11), it can be seen that the major vessels, the digital arteries, run underneath the horn on either side of the frog. This part of the foot is known as the collateral frog sulci, the deep channels which start at the heels and join up around the point of frog. One normally picks out a foot by first clearing the collateral frog sulci with a hoof pick.

This anatomical arrangement is important because;

1 The arterial blood supply to the front part of the laminar corium is solely from branches arising from the terminal arch and circumflex artery. The arterial supply to this front part of the foot plus venous and lymphatic drainage are all in an upwards direction, against gravity.

2 There is no direct arterial supply to the solar corium from the terminal arch, it all arises from inward flow from the circumflex artery.

3 There are no major arterial branches directly under the frog.

Normal anatomy

From a diagram of a normal foot split down the midline, several important relationships can be seen (Figs. 12 & 13). The phalanges [long pastern (proximal phalanx), short pastern, (middle phalanx), and pedal bone (distal phalanx)] are all in a straight line. The front surface of the pedal bone is parallel to the front of the hoof wall. The coronary corium is oval in cross-section and sits in the coronary groove at the top of the hoof. The coronary papillae are all aligned parallel to the front surface of the pedal bone. The top of the extensor process of the pedal bone is usually slightly below the top of the hoof wall. Rarely, the top of the extensor process is above the top of the hoof wall; this is normal for some animals. The horny sole is concave. The point of the frog extends in front of the insertion of the deep digital flexor tendon.

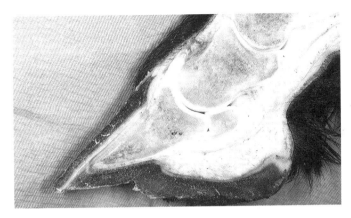

Figure 12. A normal front foot split down the centre and viewed from the cut surface.

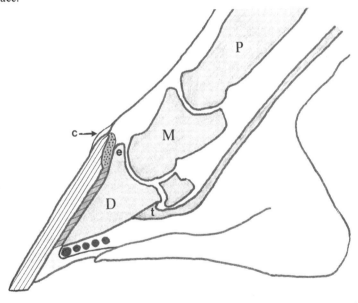

Figure 13. Diagrammatic representation of the normal split foot shown in Figure 12. Stippled area = coronary corium; hatching = laminar corium. The three phalangeal bones (P, M, & D) are in a straight line. The top of the pedal bone (e for extensor process) is slightly below the coronary band (c). The coronary corium is oval in shape, the front of the hoof wall is parallel to the front of the pedal bone. The solid dots represent the circumflex artery of the pedal bone (at the front) and blood vessels within the solar corium. Note that the frog extends in front of the area of attachment of the deep digital flexor tendon (t).

Chapter 2
WHAT HAPPENS WITHIN THE FOOT IN LAMINITIS?

It seems that the basic problem in laminitis is an interruption to the normal blood flow to the laminar corium early in the development of laminitis. Areas of laminar corium are deprived of their normal blood supply by two mechanisms a) the arteries and veins clamp down constricting the diameter of the blood vessels; and b) blood is shunted away from the tissues of the laminar corium directly into the veins. This shunting occurs via specialised vessels called arteriovenous anastomoses opening and allowing blood from the high pressure arterial side of the circulation to flow directly into the veins *without flowing through the laminar corium.* This loss of normal blood supply is known as ischaemia (*iskeemeear*). We know that it takes about four minutes for areas of the human brain to be irreparably damaged by lack of blood supply when a person has a stroke; this is the same type of damage which occurs in the laminae of a horse's foot during the early stages of laminitis. The severity of damage to the laminar corium is determined by a) the time during which ischaemia persists, and b) the area of the laminar corium which is affected.

If the blood supply is interrupted for a short time no permanent damage is likely to be done. The more severe the reduction in supply and the longer this reduction continues the greater the likelihood of irreversible changes in the laminar corium. If the blood vessels remain constricted for very long, a matter of hours, the internal lining may become damaged. Following this damage the cells lining the blood capillaries swell and tend to separate causing gaps in the blood vessel walls. Fluid from the blood then leaks out through these gaps, further increasing the already high fluid pressure in the foot. Secondarily there is a tendency for blood clots to form by sticking to the damaged cells lining the capillaries. A vessel that becomes full of blood clot is permanently occluded.

11

Why does this lack of blood supply cause such pain in laminitis? Any interruption to blood flow in this situation is painful as the laminar tissue becomes starved of oxygen and nutrients. There is evidence that further pain can occur when the blood supply is restored, this is called a reperfusion injury. **Laminitis results from lack of blood flow to the laminar corium, it is not at this stage an inflammatory disease at all.** If the blood supply is normalised fairly quickly the animal recovers with no after effects.

However if the reduction in blood supply is severe, long standing, or affects most of the laminar corium then the attachment between the pedal bone and the hoof capsule will start to fail. This occurs directly from a mechanical point of view as there is an insufficient area of healthy laminar corium left to support the pedal bone. When this situation is reached the animal is said to start to FOUNDER. We have seen that because of the anatomy of the blood supply it is the laminar corium in the front of the foot which is the most easily starved of blood. In acute founder cases, i.e. those which have occurred suddenly and recently, it is the laminar corium in this front area which is the more severely affected. As the support to the pedal bone is weakened, the initial movement of the pedal bone is downwards and backwards as the weight of the horse above overcomes the support by the damaged interlocking laminae (Fig. 14). Before the dermal and epidermal laminae are actually pulled apart they

Figure 14. Split foot of a case of acute founder (compare with Fig. 25).

become stretched. If the foot is X rayed at this stage this can be diagnosed by an increase in the distance between the front of the wall and the front of the pedal bone; this is called an increase in wall thickness. By comparing Figures 13 and 15 it can be seen that several important changes have occurred in the foundered foot. The phalangeal axis is not quite in

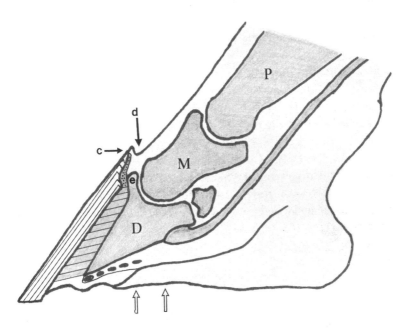

Figure 15. Diagrammatic representation of the acute founder foot in Figure 14. Stippled area = coronary corium; hatching = stretched dermal and epidermal laminae, becoming separated by leakage of fluid from blood vessels in the laminar corium; black dots = compressed circumflex artery and blood vessels in the solar corium. Note how the phalangeal bones (P, M & D) are no longer aligned. There is an increased vertical distance between the extensor process (e) and the coronary band (c), this has resulted in a squashing of the coronary corium. The downward movement of the pedal bone has created a depression at the coronary band (d ⟶) which is characteristic of acute founder and which can be felt with the fingers. The front of the pedal bone and the front of the hoof wall are no longer parallel, the space in between has filled up with serum and blood which has forced the two structures apart. The circumflex artery of the pedal bone and the blood vessels in the solar corium have become squeezed between the descending pedal bone and the horny sole which is no longer concave. Support to the pedal bone can only be provided by fitting a frog support or heart bar on the part of the frog between the two open arrows.

a straight line and the front of the pedal bone is no longer parallel to the front of the hoof capsule. The angulation between these two structures has been referred to as the angle of 'rotation' of the pedal bone. We shall see later that this angle of rotation, so often quoted, is not the only angle of rotation. In the acute founder case the separation between the bone and hoof capsule is due to the escape of fluid from the damaged laminar vessels into the spaces created by the interdigitating laminae being pulled apart. The fluid causing this separation is blood and serum (the fluid part of the blood without the cells).

The coronary corium is no longer oval in cross-section but has become compressed due to pinching between the top of the hoof wall and the front of the coffin joint. The coronary papillae are no longer aligned parallel to the front of the pedal bone. They are very bent due to the downward pull of the attached pedal bone (Fig. 16). Unless these coronary papillae can heal and re-orientate the horse will never have a normal foot again. Due to the downward movement of the pedal bone, the circumflex artery and the blood vessels of the solar corium become pinched between the underside of the pedal bone and the horny sole. This cuts off the blood supply to the solar corium and may rupture some

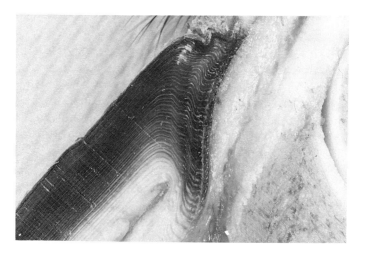

Figure 16. View of the coronary papillae in the midline from a case of acute founder. Notice how the papillae and the juvenile horn tubules have become bent by the downward movement of the pedal bone. Compare to the normal situation in Figure 7.

of the vessels in the solar corium particularly around the 'tip' of the pedal bone. If the founder gets no worse, these cases can be recognised about six weeks later by a blood stained area in the horn of the sole. This area is always crescent shaped, corresponding to the shape of the pedal bone, and is about midway between the toe and the point of frog. Additionally, the blood vessels within the laminar and coronary corium over the front of the pedal bone become stretched and often rupture during acute founder. This releases blood into the surrounding horn. In white footed animals blood from the coronary corium can be seen on the wall as a red ring which grows down the foot. Blood from ruptured vessels in the laminar corium is on the inner side of the hoof wall and tends to be seen at the white line of the toe some months later.

If the founder worsens and the pedal bone keeps descending, the horny sole becomes flattened or even convex. Thus in the acutely foundered horse, in addition to the reduction in blood supply due to laminitis, the situation is worse because the descending pedal bone has physically distorted the blood vessels. The circumflex artery of the distal phalanx and the vessels of the solar corium have become trapped between the pedal bone and the horny sole (Fig. 15). In severe cases the bone may push right through the horny sole; this is known as solar prolapse (Fig. 56). It can be appreciated that the further the pedal bone moves down, the worse the degree of founder. It is possible to tell whether a horse is foundered by feeling around his coronary bands. In the normal horse, if you run your finger down the front of the pastern, over the coronary band and onto the hoof wall, your finger slides easily. If the horse is foundered your finger tends to lodge in a ditch or depression just above the coronet. When the horse founders and the pedal bone moves down, it drags the tissues under the skin with it which creates the ditch you can feel with your finger (Fig. 15). The deeper the ditch and the farther it extends sideways around the coronet, the worse the founder (Fig. 17).

There is a special sort of founder; and it is the most serious. In some cases the blood supply to the whole of the laminar corium, right back to the heels, has been savagely starved of blood supply. In these cases the pedal bone becomes detached from the hoof capsule all the way round the foot as all the laminar corium is affected. The pedal bone is loose within the hoof; these cases are known as SINKERS (Fig 18). The coronary papillae are bent, not just in the front part of the foot but right back to the heels. The pedal bone is no longer suspended by the laminae

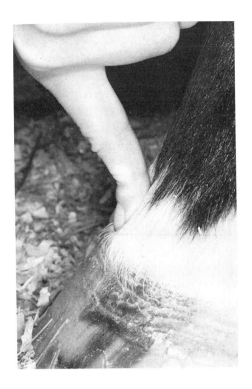

Figure 17. How to feel for the depression at the coronary band indicative of acute founder or sinker syndrome. Run the finger lightly down the pastern and over the coronary band onto the hoof wall. There is no resistance to this procedure in the normal animal: in a case of acute founder or sinker syndrome the finger tends to lodge in a depression as shown in the figure.

but is resting on the inside of the horny sole thus cutting off the blood flow to the solar and laminar corium. In these cases the ditch extends all the way around the coronet from one heel to the other. There is only a matter of hours in which to attempt to save most of these cases. However, if the correct treatment is provided in time, within a few hours, they can be cured and return to working lives.

Healing

Laminitis cases, although they may be in acute pain temporarily, should respond to treatment and be left with no permanent changes in the feet. Founder cases will be left with some degree of foot distortion if corrective treatment is not provided. Even if treatment is provided some unresponsive cases will show a degree of hoof abnormality characteristic of CHRONIC FOUNDER. Chronic means of 'long standing' i.e. the

Figure 18. The coronary papillae and juvenile horn tubules are severely bent in this case of sinker syndrome. Compare to Figures 7 & 16. Although this tissue has been taken from the midline, in a sinker the same deformation would be shown by coronary papillae at the heels.

opposite of acute. 'Chronic' infers nothing about the severity of the condition. These changes are directly attributable to the movement of the pedal bone within the hoof. The toe of the foot tends to elongate, the front wall may become curved and the heels of the foot grow more quickly than the toe (Fig. 19). Additionally, the coronary band appears less distinct than normal; the hoof wall seems to merge with the skin. The white line of the foot becomes stretched or wider than normal around the toe of the foot. The sole of the foot may appear flat or dropped i.e. lower than the hoof wall at the ground surface. When the pedal bone moves down the coronary papillae may become permanently damaged leading to a reduced rate of growth compared with the unaffected part of the coronary corium at the heels. This can be seen easily if the animal has growth rings on the hoof walls. If a horse has foundered the rings will be wider at the heels than the toe. (*It is important to differentiate between the growth rings of chronic founder and those of a change in diet. Chronic founder rings are divergent, i.e. wider at the heels than the toe whereas the rings caused by a change in feeding are the same width all the way round the foot.*) When the two sets of laminae are pulled apart, the

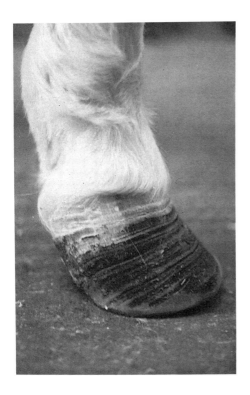

Figure 19. A foot showing the classical changes of chronic founder, high heels, concave front wall and divergent growth rings. Many of these types of case can be dramatically improved by correct foot trimming and shoeing.

surface of the healing laminae may be altered leading to an abnormally high rate of production of laminar horn which grows straight forwards leading to the elongating toe and stretched white line. This alteration to the laminae is **not** always permanent. Flattening of the sole is due to the new, lower position of the pedal bone within the hoof. This flattening of the sole can be reversed in many cases by surgical treatment to the deep digital flexor tendon and heart bar shoeing.

From the foregoing, it is possible for you and your vet to tell the difference between a case of LAMINITIS, ACUTE FOUNDER, SINKING or CHRONIC FOUNDER just by looking at the feet. It is important that these different types of the basic condition are recognised as each carries a different prognosis and each can be expected to respond to treatments differently. Prognosis means the prediction of the outcome following treatment i.e. whether the animal will be cured or not. Treatment that consists of a balanced combination of medical, farriery and possibly surgical approaches has the best chance of success. The sooner correct treatment is started the better the chance of recovery. Prompt treatment is mandatory for the more severe forms, the acute founder and sinker cases. I will begin by describing the foot treatments that are recommended for each type of case.

Chapter 3
THE AIMS OF FOOT TREATMENTS, SHOEING AND SURGICAL TREATMENTS

1. Laminitis Cases

As it is not possible to tell whether a laminitis case is going to deteriorate and founder, it is sensible to treat them all as if they might. The aim of foot treatments is to try and counteract the downward movement of the pedal bone. Nothing should be placed under the horny sole because a) the sole of the foot is not designed to bear weight, in fact it will bruise and abscess if forced to do so, and b) there is nowhere on the sole that support could be applied to achieve a mechanical advantage. By referring to Figure 15 it can be seen that the only place where a supporting influence can be provided to the pedal bone is between the two open arrows under the frog. Pushing further forward than the front arrow would not support the pedal bone but rather extend the coffin joint; pushing further back than the back arrow tends to flex the coffin joint and make the pedal bone tilt more. Any form of frog support must only be applied within the margins of the trimmed frog; pressure elsewhere risks damage to the arteries under the horn (Fig. 11). Only by X-raying the foot can we get an appreciation of the relative positions of the structures in the foot. At this point it would be as well to describe how X-rays should be taken.

X-ray technique

A few simple preliminaries will make the difference between an X-ray that is some use for diagnostic and prognostic purposes and one which is not. A wooden block is needed about 3 inches high and wide enough for the horse to stand on. A cut-off bicycle spoke is embedded into the top of the wooden block to highlight the ground line. The horse's foot is picked and brushed out and any flaking horn or shaggy frog trimmed away. It is important to trim the frog so that the collateral sulci can be seen to their depths on both sides of the frog which are then bevelled. The frog does not show up well on lateral X-rays, in order to show the frog in relation to the pedal bone inside, a marker (usually a drawing pin) is used to highlight the frog. The pin is pushed into the front inch of the frog. It does not matter exactly where the pin is placed as long as its position on the frog is marked in some way. I prefer to draw a felt tipped pen line right across the sole and frog. Then reference can be made back to the frog following examination of the X-ray (Fig. 20).

For prognostic purposes when X-raying laminitis, acute founder and sinker cases, another marker is used on the front of the hoof wall. This time a straight stiff wire with square ends and of known length (about 55 mm long) is used to highlight the front and top of the hoof wall. It is important to know the length of the wire so that the effects of magnification in taking the X-ray can be allowed for. Firstly the top of the

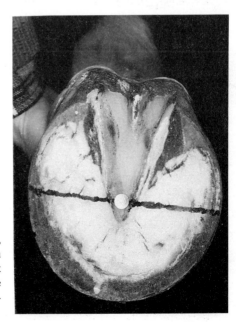

Figure 20. Prior to taking an X-ray, the frog is trimmed and a drawing pin with a shortened point is placed about 1 cm back from the point of frog. The position of the pin is marked by drawing a line across the frog and sole.

hoof wall just below the coronary band is lightly rasped to remove flaking or excessive perioplic horn. The top of the wall in the midline is gently pushed with your finger and the top of the wire marker sellotaped to the wall with the top of the wire where the wall starts to yield into softer perioplic horn (Fig 21). The position where the top of the wire was placed may be marked with an indelible pen.

The horse should ideally stand with one foot on the block with the cannon bone vertical, this doesn't happen very often in practice so we usually have to lift the other leg. The X-ray beam should be parallel to the top of the block and perpendicular to the axis of the limb so that an absolutely sideways-on X-ray picture is produced (Fig. 22).

Frog supports

A variety of materials can be used to make frog supports, triangles of carpet, rubber, leather or plastic can be stuck to the frog or held in place

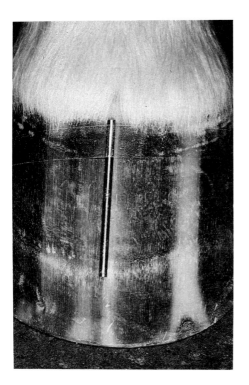

Figure 21. In addition to the pin marker a piece of straight stiff wire about 55 mm long is sellotaped to the front of the wall of the foot. THE TOP OF THE WIRE IS PLACED WHERE THE HORN CHANGES FROM HARD TO SOFT. It is sometimes necessary to lightly rasp the wall to smooth the horn before fitting the wire marker.

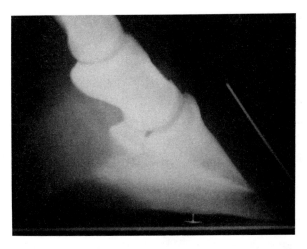

Figure 22. X-ray of a normal foot, compare with Figure 12. The phalanges are in a straight line, the wire marker is parallel to the front of the pedal bone, the top of the wire is in a normal position just above the top of the pedal bone and the pedal bone is at a normal angle to the ground.

with an Elastoplast type bandage. (Remember not to bandage over the coronary band and to pad the heels with cotton wool to avoid rubs.) Because the materials used to make frog supports are fairly soft it is not necessary to X-ray the foot prior to fitting them provided they are fitted within the margins of the frog. The idea of a frog support is like an arch support in your shoe. It should not be so thick so the horse has to take most of his weight on it; this would make him much more lame. Figures 23 & 24 show how a frog support made of a roll of bandage is fitted. The horse was then walked along a black mat. The density of blackening roughly shows the relative weight bearing. A commercially produced type of frog support known as a Lily Pad is available. These often have to be trimmed extensively to fit and can make the heels of the horse sore after a few days.

2. Acute Founder Cases

Although the frog supports are quite satisfactory as temporary measures, up to a week, founder cases will need more permanent and stronger forms of frog support known as heart bar shoes. A variety of

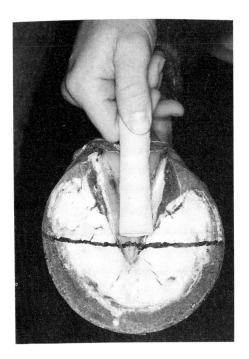

Figure 23. Fitting a frog support made of a part roll of bandage. The bandage is unrolled until it is the correct thickness for the individual foot, then it is placed along the axis of the frog with the front end of the roll about 1 cm behind the **trimmed** point of frog. . .

styles of heart bar shoes is available. The farrier can only make a heart bar shoe fit properly if the feet have been X-rayed in the manner previously described (Fig. 25). NO FORM OF HEART BAR SHOE SHOULD BE FITTED WITHOUT MARKED X-RAYS HAVING BEEN TAKEN.

The **non-adjustable steel heart bar shoe** is shown in Figure 26. The heart bar shoe is a precision instrument being made to fit each foot individually. The essential feature of the shoe is that, during fitting, the heart bar contacts the frog before the branches of the shoe touch the walls of the foot. Thus the shoe exerts pressure on the frog when it is nailed on even before weight bearing occurs. The amount of support provided by the shoe is judged before nailing on by pressing the shoe firmly to the foot. If the horse resents this there is too much pressure from the heart bar which should be hammered back a little and the test repeated. Like all nailed on shoes it suffers from the major disadvantage that most sore-

Figure 24. Making sure the roll of bandage does not twist across the frog, it is taped to the foot by means of elastic adhesive tape. Be careful not to tape tightly over the coronary band and remember to pad the heels with Gamgee or cotton wool. This horse has been walked along a black mat, the intensity of the black colouration is proportional to the loading of the various parts of the foot. Most of the load is on the wall, none on the sole and the frog now acts as an arch support.

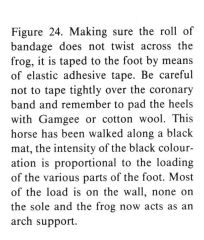

footed horses resent nailing on. The adjustment of this sort of shoe is thus a little hit and miss. However it provides a strong means of frog support when fitted.

An **all-steel adjustable heart bar shoe** was developed in the USA (Fig. 27). In this design the base of the heart bar (the piece which covers the frog) is hinged at the heels. A bar is welded between quarter and quarter and is drilled and tapped to accept a grub screw. By turning the grub screw with an Allen key the heart bar is raised or lowered thereby altering the amount of frog support. This type of shoe again has the disadvantage of being nailed on but the advantage of being able to perform the adjustment when the shoe is on the foot.

The shoe which was developed and is used routinely at The Laminitis Clinic is a plastic and steel glue-on adjustable heart bar shoe (**Eustace shoe**) (Fig. 28). This has the advantage of being glued to the foot, the shoe can be made and fitted with the horse lying down, if necessary.

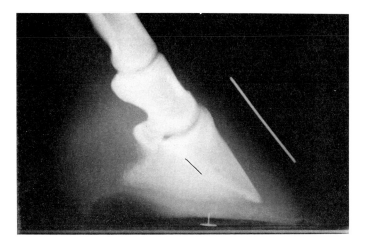

Figure 25. An X-ray of an early case of acute founder. The pedal bone has started to move down and backwards within the foot (compare with Figure 22) as shown by an increased vertical distance between the top of the wire and the top of the pedal bone (see Figure 54). There is a loss of parallelism between the wire and the front of the pedal bone.

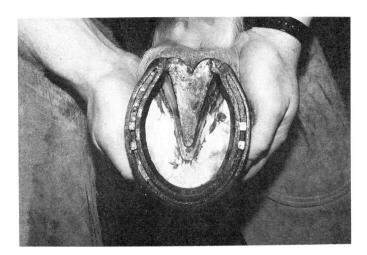

Figure 26. A good example of an all steel non-adjustable heart bar shoe correctly fitted. The shoe is fitted with the minimum of nails, the shoe is well seated to avoid the shoe pressing on the sole, the toe is rolled and the shoe has been fitted with sufficient length and width at the heels. Most importantly no part of the heart bar extends outside of the margins of the trimmed frog.

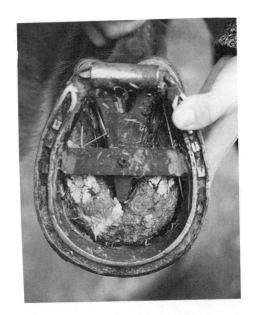

Figure 27. An all steel adjustable heart bar shoe. The heart bar is hinged at the base. The shoe is fitted with no pressure on the heart bar. Frog support is increased after nailing on by turning the grub screw (near the centre of the foot) with an Allen key.

Strong, constant and adjustable frog support is achieved by turning an Allen key in the same way as the previous shoe. Nailing shoes to the feet of very lame horses is no longer mandatory with the advent of the glue-shoe technology.

Another form of all **plastic heart bar shoe** is available. However this has the major disadvantage of there being little control over the amount of frog support which in any case is only acting when the horse stands on the shoe. When he lifts his foot, the frog support is removed.

3. Sinkers

These cases need to be treated by means of a frog support shoe, preferably a Eustace shoe, within a few hours of sinking if the horse is to have any sort of chance of becoming sound again. As we have seen, all the laminal attachments have been destroyed in a sinker and the pedal bone is sitting on the bottom of the hoof capsule (Fig. 29). Unless the pedal bone can be lifted (or the hoof capsule dragged down) to restore the normal relationship between the pedal bone and the hoof, i.e. straighten the coronary papillae and remove the pressure on the circumflex artery and

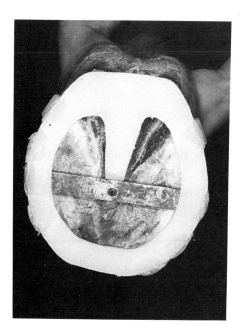

Figure 28. The plastic and steel glue-on adjustable heart bar shoe (Eustace shoe) developed at the Laminitis Clinic. The shoe is adjusted in the same way as that in Figure 27 but is attached to the foot by means of glue rather than nails. Shoeing with this device has proven to be less traumatic to both the horse and the farrier!

vessels of the solar corium, the horse will have to be destroyed. This normalising of the anatomy is only possible for a short few hours after sinking because as time progresses there is haemorrhage and gross swelling of the laminar corium which prevents movement of the bone within the hoof. If this stage has been reached there is a real possibility of the hooves dropping off. This may happen very quickly with the pedal bones of all four feet penetrating the soles within 36 hours or it may take several weeks before the hooves detach.

Surgical treatments for acute founder cases

Having addressed ourselves to the bottom of the foot and the problems of a descending pedal bone in founder and sinker cases, there is the area of the fluid-soaked laminae below the front part of the hoof wall to be discussed. In the early stages of founder considerable volumes of serum fluid can accumulate under the front wall of the hoof. This has leaked from the damaged blood vessels in the laminar corium. Additionally

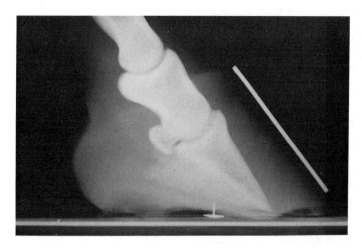

Figure 29. X-ray of a foot of a sinker. The founder distance (between the top of the pedal bone and the top of the wire, see Fig. 54) is greatly increased from normal (compare with Fig. 22) and the tip of the pedal bone is resting on the inside of the horny sole causing it to become convex. This pony was destroyed.

there may be areas of haemorrhage from the same source. This fluid can in some cases build up considerable hydrostatic pressure under the wall of the hoof. The human analogy would be the blood blister under the finger nail, exquisitely painful until the pressure is released by burning through the nail with a red hot needle. The difference is that the fluid under the horses hoof wall is not usually in one nice big pocket, rather it is compartmentalized by the leaf-like laminae. X-rays are of no help to decide whether there is fluid trapped under the hoof wall as fluid does not show up on X-rays. The only way to decide in a case of *acute founder* is to drill a hole through the hoof wall near the midline about one third of the way up the wall. This must be done carefully, of course, to avoid drilling too deeply and into the laminar corium. If a pocket of fluid is entered the pressure may be so great as to spurt out of the drill hole. Drainage of a substantial pocket of fluid will give the horse great relief. If no fluid is released, an iodine cotton wool soaked swab can be used to plug the hole and no damage will have been done. This is known as DORSAL WALL DRILLING. Dorsal, in this situation means 'the front of'. When there is a large accumulation of fluid and the front of the pedal bone is no longer attached to the inside of the hoof wall, it will be best to extend the dorsal wall drill hole into a DORSAL WALL RESECTION (removal of the front hoof wall) (Fig. 30). This will allow release of pressure on the laminar corium in the front of the foot, removal of dead laminar tissue and drainage of any infection which may have developed. The dorsal wall resection also allows the new coronary horn to grow down and remain parallel to the front of the pedal bone. (Remember that coronary horn grows in tubules so new horn has to follow the old. If the old horn is no longer parallel to the pedal bone it is better to remove it and allow new growth to assume the correct direction.)

A dorsal wall resection can be done with a sharp hoof knife and half curved hoof nippers. However an electrically driven high speed milling (Dremel) tool is necessary to make a tidy job and to remove the horn closest to the laminar corium with delicacy. This procedure does not

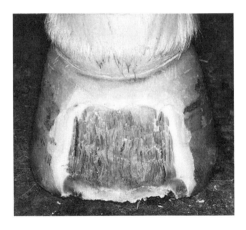

Figure 30. This foot is at the old founder stage. The first part of the dorsal wall resection operation has been performed by removing the bulk of the wall horn with half-curved nippers. This pony showed no discomfort during the procedure which has exposed the leaf-like epidermal laminae. These are longer than normal and soaking wet with serum. Notice a 'waist' in the hoof wall, just below the coronary band. The horn above this line has grown since the pony foundered following re-alignment of the coronary papillae. The new horn is much 'tighter' around the pedal bone because the old stretched laminae are being pushed down the foot by the new horn growth. I usually leave the resection at this stage for 48 hours to dry out. The laminar horn is then much more easily removed with an electric milling tool.

require a general anaesthetic nor a local anaesthetic as live tissue is not being cut. Most cases do not even need a tranquilliser. The occasional animal is irritated by the noise of the drill or tickled by horn shavings flying onto the pastern.

Abscesses

It is not uncommon for abscesses to form in the feet of acutely foundered horses. They can occur up to three months after the initial onset of founder, during their formation and until they are either drained or they burst, the horse is very lame on the affected leg(s). Abscesses occur in areas of dead or dying laminar or solar corium, between the pedal bone and the hoof capsule. These abscesses often start as pockets of haemorrhage or serum accumulation which are invaded by bacteria from the surviving blood supply at the periphery of the pocket. If this occurs in the front part of the foot the situation can be dealt with relatively easily by performing a dorsal wall drilling or resection and draining the affected area. Even if the abscess is located in the solar corium in the front part of the foot it is better to drain it via a dorsal wall resection than by making a hole in the horny sole. This is because the solar corium of foundered horses tends to swell and protrude through the hole in the sole. Such tissue can then take many weeks to heal and form new solar horn.

If, however, the abscess arises in the back part of the foot, in the laminar, solar or frog corium, the situation is less easily remedied. Attempts at direct drainage should be resisted; one never finds a pocket of infection. Rather, the foot should be tubbed in hot water at least six times a day to encourage the infection to erupt. The coronary bands on the heels and the back of the foot should be kept moist with an udder cream type ointment. Eventually the abscess will burst, usually above the bulbs of the heels and the lameness improves. Very occasionally the abscess may burst internally into an important synovial structure like the navicular bursa or the coffin joint. This unfortunately is the end of the day and time to cease treatment.

Most abscesses burst to the outside and, although painful for the horse at the time, do not worsen the long term prognosis. There is no point in treating the horse with antibiotics at this stage, if they do anything at all antibiotics will just temporarily retard eruption of the abscess. Pus in a horse's foot will only resolve by drainage. The horse should be vaccinated against tetanus.

4. Old Founder Cases

Another stage of the founder process can be described between acute and chronic founder. This can be called 'old founder' and represents a stage at which the foundered horse is not deteriorating further, i.e. the bone is no longer descending and the tissues of the foot are starting to heal. These cases are usually over the worst of their lameness by this time. When the feet of these cases are X-rayed a black area can often be seen under the hoof wall or under the sole (Figs. 31 & 32) This indicates the presence of gas. The gas may be air that has entered the foot from the outside through a crack in the white line or it may have

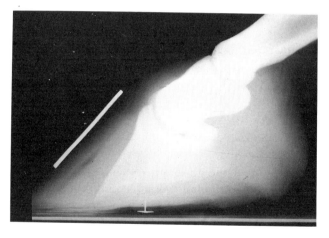

Figure 31. X-ray of a front foot of an Arab mare at the old founder stage, 7 weeks after the acute founder. In this case the founder distance is small, within the normal range, the coronary tissues have remodelled and reduced the founder distance. There is a linear gas shadow under the hoof wall. This indicates that a small pocket of fluid has been resorbed, some abnormal laminar horn has started to form from the damaged laminar corium. This is evidenced by the gas shadow being so close under the hoof wall; generally the closer the shadow to the hoof wall (as opposed to being close to the bone) the longer the time since the acute founder stage. The mare became sound.

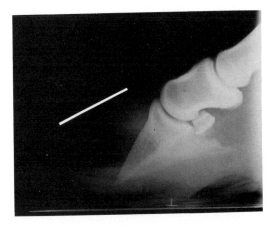

Figure 32. Another case at the old founder stage, this time a cob gelding. This foot shows a very large gas shadow extending around the foot to the quarters. This owners of this cob had been badly advised and the horse neglected. Following extensive reconstructive work the horse made a full recovery.

been produced internally by bacteria acting on a pocket of serum or haemorrhage. Gas between the hoof wall and pedal bone means that a dorsal wall resection is indicated. You do not expect to release any fluid from an old founder foot; most of that has been resorbed into the foot and the areas filled by gas. However, some serum or blood-soaked dead laminar tissue can be removed and the overlying old wall removed ready for the growth of the new coronary horn.

The remaining strength of the attachment between the hoof and the corium following founder will determine the need for specialist foot treatments and shoeing. Although this does not alter the prognosis of the case it can prolong the treatment period and may incur more expense. In some cases at the old founder stage most of the hoof capsule will have only very weak connections with the corium. If this occurs it is often better to remove this old hoof capsule and either leave the animal unshod in a deeply bedded stable or build it a new hoof using artificial horn materials. Note this is at the *old founder* stage, when any solar prolapse has healed and formed new solar horn (Figs. 33 & 34). If this procedure, which can be called a wall resection, is not done there is independent movement between the old hoof and the corium and new

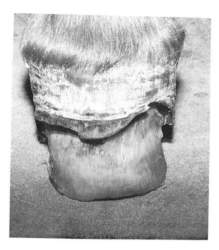

Figure 33. Similarly to the situation of the cob in Figure 32, when the old hoof capsule becomes so detached from underlying corium and new horn that it moves largely independently, the animal is often more comfortable if it is removed. This allows the new horn to grow closely down around the pedal bone instead of being pulled away at every stride. This is the same animal as in Fig. 8, the pedal bone had penetrated the sole in this foot and in the other feet which were treated similarly.

horn. This results in squeezing or pinching at the coronary band which causes pain to the horse.

Other surgical treatments for founder and sinker cases

In some cases of founder another complicating factor may start to operate. The muscle which works the deep digital flexor tendon starts to work overtime and contract. The reasons for this are unknown but may be related to the animal's individual pain threshold and the founder distance. As the muscle contracts the pedal bone is pulled more and more away from the inside of the hoof wall (Figs. 35 & 36). This is painful to the animal as the laminal attachments are physically torn apart. The pull on the pedal bone forces it to tilt or rotate and results in pain in the coffin joint due to malalignment of the pedal bone and the short pastern bone. Once this process starts it rarely stops. Mechanical release of tension on the deep flexor tendon can be obtained by raising the heels of the foot. However, this is **not** at all recommended in an acute founder

Figure 34. The same foot as in Figure 33 five months later. The pony made a full recovery and is sound without shoes. A plastic glue-on bar shoe with lateral extension has been fitted to help the foot grow back in balance.

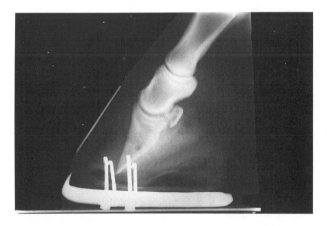

Figure 35. An X-ray of the right fore foot of the pony in Figure 36 at the old founder stage, see the black gas shadows under the wire marker. Notice how the pedal bone has become tilted out of alignment with the proximal phalanges by the pull of the deep digital flexor tendon. Incidentally, see how by leaving the nail heads proud of the fullering in the shoe this has tilted the shoe onto the heels. This is a bad practice not only in terms of laminitis but also relating to navicular syndrome.

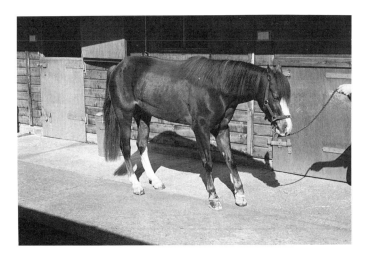

Figure 36. This pony has foundered in all four feet and is now at the old founder stage. Although superficially the pony appears to be adopting a classical laminitis stance with the forelegs stretched out in front; closer inspection shows the pony to be standing on its **toes** rather than its **heels**. This condition is due to excessive deep digital flexor tendon strain which can only be corrected by cutting the tendon (see Figs 37 & 39).

or sinker case as even more compression is being placed on the coronary corium in the front of the foot and the pedal bone is likely to 'slide down' the laminae and drastically worsen the founder. The alternative method of treatment is to surgically cut the deep digital flexor tendon. This can give instant relief in suitable cases and if done on sinker or acute founder cases can return them to normality (Fig. 37). The operation can be performed under local anaesthetic in the standing animal through a cut, too small to need stitching (Fig. 38). The two ends of the tendon are not stitched together and in fact they often spring apart by up to an inch. The tendon ends send out new tendon fibres to bridge the gap; this can occur in about three months. This new tendon is juvenile and the horse should be rested for a year before putting strain on the new tendon. These cases need to be fitted with Eustace shoes with posterior extensions at the time of the operation. This is necessary to help foot placement on uneven bedding and prevent over-extension of the coffin joint. This style of shoeing will be necessary for three months during which time the animal should not be turned out loose. It can be walked out in hand on

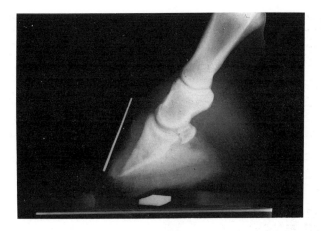

Figure 37. The same foot as in Figure 35 six days later, the deep digital flexor tendon has been cut in the interim. The phalanges are all back in alignment, the heels of the foot have been lowered to set the angle of the pedal bone correctly in relation to the ground. A dorsal wall resection has also been performed and a Eustace shoe fitted.

smooth ground. Free exercise is inadvisable for at least 6 months. Provided the deep digital flexor tendon is cut at the correct time, i.e. when contracture is noticed but before irreversible damage is done to the coronary corium through compression, the animal can return to a normal life of riding or driving work after a year's rest (Fig. 39).

In some cases in which there appears to be an abnormally strong pull from the deep flexor tendon, yet not enough to warrant cutting it, another operation can be performed. This involves removing the inferior check ligament. This is a short fibrous structure connecting the deep flexor tendon to the back of the top of the knee and cannon bone. It is hard to rationalise why this operation should work; in practice this seems to give more laxity to the flexor tendon and reduce the pull. A general anaesthetic is needed for this operation.

5. Chronic Founder Cases (Types 1 & 2)

I have described the changes in the horse's foot which characterise chronic founder. Many acute founder cases will develop these changes to a variable extent. When faced with such a foot there is a limit to what

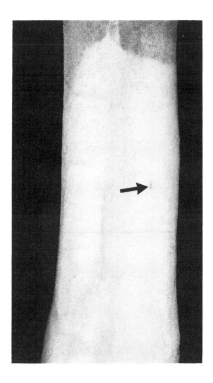

Figure 38. This shows the site for cutting the deep flexor tendon in the mid cannon region. This leg was clipped for surgery and operated on 10 days previously. The surgical wound is arrowed.

the veterinary surgeon or farrier can do to 'cure' the animal. However, by correct foot dressing and shoeing the gait of these animals can be greatly improved and they can often lead a pain-free and productive life.

The aim of foot treatment in the chronic founder case is to restore the relationship between the phalangeal bones, the hoof and the ground to as near normality as possible. We have seen that chronic founder cases tend to produce an excess of laminar horn around the front part of their feet and grow their heels faster than their toes. This tends to force the pedal bone into an ever more tilted or 'rotated' position. The farrier must compensate for this by removing rather more heel than toe; the exact amount can be judged by looking at the relative widths of the growth rings. **Most importantly, the front wall must be rasped back to keep it parallel with the front of the pedal bone inside.** This often means in neglected or long standing cases that the front wall proper, the tubular horn produced by the coronary corium, must the rasped right through

Figure 39. The same pony as in Figure 36 two months later, able to adopt a normal stance and on the way to a full recovery for ridden work.

to expose the laminar horn underneath. In many chronic founder cases this laminar horn is produced relentlessly, because of alterations to the laminar corium which occurred at the time of founder, the laminar horn is in fact under pressure. The horn is compressed between the harder outer tubular wall horn and the front of the pedal bone inside.

When the outer wall is rasped through it is common to see the laminar horn 'expand' or unwrap and become proud of the level of the wall horn around it. This pressure in the front of a chronic foundered foot causes discomfort, making the horse walk on the heels, which are already overgrown. By keeping the feet dressed in this manner, at least every six weeks, the phalangeal axis is kept straight and the pedal bone is at a normal angulation (about ten degrees) to the ground. It is sometimes not easy for the farrier to be sure how much of the front wall must be rasped away to restore parallelism with the front of the pedal bone. An excellent guide is to look at the foot from the side and study the angulation of the most recent horn, just below the coronary band at the front (Fig. 40). If this line is extended to the ground and all the horn in front is rasped away the remaining wall will be within two degrees of parallelism with the front of the pedal bone inside (Fig. 41). The farrier should ask for an X-ray to be taken if he is not sure how much to rasp back. Farriers

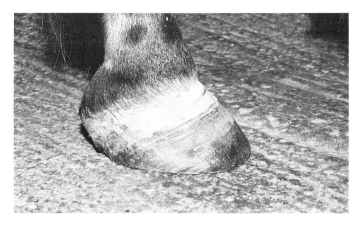

Figure 40. A chronic founder Type 1 foot. This foot would look longer with a concave front wall rather than a convex one if someone had not nibbled at the toe with a rasp. The most recently produced horn, about the top inch, just below the coronary band is at a much more upright angle than the rest of the front wall. If this line is extended to the ground removing all the horn in front, the remaining wall will be within 2 degrees of parallelism to the front of the bone inside (see Fig. 41).

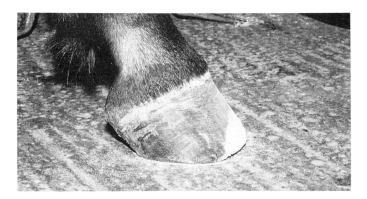

Figure 41. Same foot as in previous Figure 10 minutes later. Rasping back the toe has exposed a crescent of the abnormal whitish laminar horn so characteristic of chronic founder cases. This animal was much more comfortable after this foot dressing, it must be like having a pair of clogs replaced by running shoes!

refer to this rasping of the front wall of the foot as 'dressing the foot forwards'.

There are some chronic founder cases with very high heels which, when one sees them should ring warning bells. These are often long standing cases which have developed deep digital flexor tendon contracture. The pedal bone is kept in a tilted position by the pull of the deep digital flexor tendon. If a lot of heel is suddenly removed from these cases they are likely to be more lame and may even be unable to put their heels on the ground. The only way to improve these cases is to cut the deep digital flexor tendon. It is possible to test for these animals by using a simple test. Before much heel horn is removed a crescent-shaped wedge is placed under the toe; this has the same effect as lowering the heels. If the animal is more uncomfortable with the toe wedge in place and the other limb lifted it is likely that the flexor tendon is involved and it would be unwise to lower the heels without full discussion between owner, farrier and veterinary surgeon. When using the wedge test, be sure that the wedge is not placed under the sole and the animal made to stand on it as this will make it more uncomfortable whether the tendon is involved or not. Either use a crescentic wedge which only bears around the hoof wall or perform the test while the foot is shod. The types of chronic founder cases just described, whether the flexor tendon is involved or not, I refer to as Type 1 (Figs. 42 & 43).

Chronic founder Type 2

There is another type of case which develops the same type of foot distortion as in the chronic founder Type 1 yet is mortally affected; these cases I call a chronic founder Type 2. The essential difference between the two types is that the Type 1 animals can lead almost pain-free lives whilst the Type 2 cases remain severely lame from the time they founder or sink. Type 2 cases only have a life expectancy of up to three years. That is three years as a cripple before someone finally puts them down on humane grounds. There may be intermittent periods of relative improvement in the level of lameness these animals show. The periods of most severe lameness are associated with the build up of serum pockets which may then progress to form abscesses. These are usually under the sole around the tip of the pedal bone and will erupt periodically through the sole or by migration up the wall and out of the coronary band. The serum pockets form because there is an abnormal and permanently

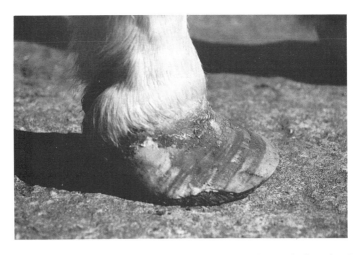

Figure 42. An old Sheltand pony's foot, an example of chronic founder Type 1 (see Fig. 43).

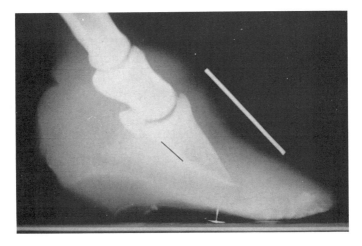

Figure 43. X-ray of the foot in Figure 42. The phalangeal alignment is not straight but easily corrected by lowering the heels. The toe is overgrown, but see how the new horn in the top half of the foot is nearly parallel with the front of the pedal bone this is characteristic of chronic founder Type 1 cases. The dark line indicates the area of insertion of the deep digital flexor tendon. Importantly, the drawing pin was placed 1 cm behind the point of frog *without first trimming the frog.* If the apex of a heart bar shoe had been fitted at the pin mark on this foot without bothering to take this X-ray, the bar would be too far forward and might easily have caused the tip of the pedal bone to fracture!

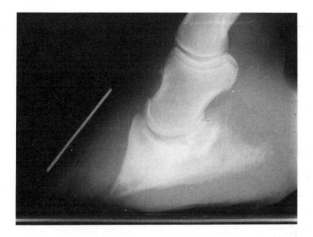

Figure 44. X-ray of chronic founder Type 2 foot. See how much of the pedal bone has disappeared (compare to Figure 43). The tip of the pedal bone is just under a sole ulcer, it is not covered by horn just by granulating solar corium. Also the overgrown toe is a solid wedge of laminar horn right up to the coronary band. This horse was destroyed.

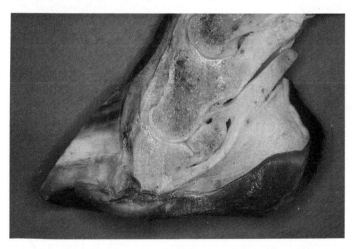

Figure 45. Split foot: Chronic founder Type 2. A very similar foot to that in the previous figure. This foot is grossly abnormal, compare to Figure 12. The distal half of the pedal bone has been resorbed, the bone is resting on the inside of the horny sole resulting in continual bruising and abscessation. Close examination shows that the coronary groove has become stretched and is in fact longer than the laminar corium! With so little laminar corium left there is no wonder that the horse cannot be supported within this hoof capsule (see Fig. 46).

Figure 46. Close up view of the coronary groove area in Figure 45. The horn tubules from the coronary corium are pointing nearly horizontally instead of down the wall parallel to the front of the pedal bone (compare with Figure 7). There is also a wave or crimp in the horn tubules which is typical of chronic founder Type 2 cases at this stage of the disease. The crimp is caused by chronic instability of the pedal bone within the hoof capsule.

distorted circulation in the foot. In addition the pedal bone to some extent rests on the inside of the horny sole because there is insufficient support from the laminae. This leads to chronic bruising of the sole with intermittent formation of serum pockets or abscesses. The pedal bone itself is much smaller than normal and the 'tip' looks ragged on X-ray (Fig. 44). This is because when the pedal bone is not subject to the normal suspending pull from the laminal attachments it is absorbed into the blood stream; this is known as absolute disuse atrophy. Another reason for part of the pedal bone to disappear is because it is being pressed onto the inside of the horny sole; this is known as pressure atrophy (Figs. 45 & 46). In some cases there may be osteomyelitis or pus-like infection of the bone itself. This is painful for the horse and a very difficult complication to try and treat.

If the feet of a chronic founder Type 2 case are dressed i.e. trimmed according to the recommendations for a Type 1, the speed of founder can increase. This is because the pedal bone in a Type 2 case is weakly held up by a mass of abnormal laminar horn onto the inside of the wall. If the foot has grown very long and much toe is removed to restore the parallelism between the front of the pedal bone and the front of the hoof wall, a significant part of the already weak support will be removed. This can result in the bone starting to sag down within the hoof more quickly than previously. The horny sole becomes more and more convex, depressions deepen at the coronary bands and pockets of serum develop under the sole. This scenario is untreatable and the animal should be put down.

Chapter 4
MEDICAL TREATMENTS

The medical treatments used on a case of laminitis fall into three basic groups;

1) Pain killing drugs,
2) Drugs which dilate the blood vessels in the foot, and
3) Anti blood clotting drugs.

The pain killing drugs of most value are the Non Steroidal Anti Inflammatory Drugs (NSAIDs) of which there are four in common usage for horses. The most common and cheapest is phenylbutazone (bute); this is available as a powder or a paste and is sold under various trade names such as, Equipalazone and ProDynam. It is also available as an injection for intravenous use only (it is very irritant to the tissues if injected outside the vein) and sold as Tomanol and Phenyzone. The second drug is meclofenamate and is sold as granules under the trade names of Arquel or Equafen. At the time of writing an injectable form is not available. Flunixin meglumine is the third drug sold as Finadyne. I have not found this drug as effective a pain killer for laminitis as the other two but its use should be considered for animals which are ill in themselves (systemically ill) or are infected as well as having laminitis. This is because flunixin has an action against some of the toxic products produced by bacteria, the endotoxins. The fourth drug is common-or-garden aspirin, or salicylate. Aspirin is a moderately good pain killer but has an action to help prevent platelets in the blood clumping together. This clumping is part of the blood clotting process and is an undesirable secondary effect in digital vessels following periods of constriction in the early stages of laminitis. As pain killers the NSAIDs have an indirect effect of reducing the animal's blood pressure which tends to rise largely in response to pain. This reduction in blood pressure is a good thing; the longer the horse has been in laminitic pain the less effective the drugs are at reducing the animal's blood pressure.

The danger with the NSAID's is overdosage. These drugs can cause ulceration and bleeding from the bowel, which may prove fatal if too much drug is given or the correct amount is given for too long. These side effects are worse for ponies and are more likely to occur in elderly animals. Thus it is important to use the least amount of drug necessary to achieve the required amount of pain relief. The other problem with the use of NSAIDs for laminitis is that because they are pain killers they can mask how lame an animal really is. This tempts people to allow the horse more exercise than is good for it. By the same token, because the animal has less painful feet he is prepared to exercise more and lie down less. This puts more mechanical strain on the laminae and increases the risk of founder starting.

The second group of drugs, the vasodilators, or blood vessel relaxing drugs can be used in combination with the NSAIDs. The most useful of the vasodilators, particularly in the early stages of laminitis, is phenoxy-benzamine, sold as Dibenyline. Unfortunately, the drug is not licensed for use in horses in the UK. Nevertheless it can stop deterioration of a laminitis case by normalising the blood supply and thus removing the pain. It is available as an injection but must be diluted in sterile saline solution and given as an intravenous drip over a period of an hour. Phenoxybenzamine has a marked tranquillising side effect so the dose is split and half given 24 or 48 hours after the initial dose. The drug is very effective at lowering the blood pressure and this can cause problems of shock in very sick or dehydrated animals. Animals often lie down and rest after this drug so they must be in a clean, well bedded stable. The fact that the horse's weight is off the feet is also a beneficial effect of this treatment.

Acepromazine (ACP) is a commonly used tranquillizing drug. It is available as tablets, a paste or by injection. It is nowhere near as effective as phenoxybenzamine as a vasodilator but can be a useful part of the treatment regime. ACP does reduce the animal's anxiety whilst having a mild vasodilator action and reducing the blood pressure. ACP is given at sufficient dosage to produce a mild tranquillizing effect. *If phenoxyben-zamine is unavailable then the use of ACP, a NSAID and frog support is recommended as the first line of treatment for laminitis cases.*

Isoxsuprine is another drug which is used to dilate the blood vessels in the feet, it has been used for the treatment of navicular disease in combination with correct shoeing. It is available as a paste (Circulon), capsules (Duviculine) and as a powder. Although this drug is unlikely to do any harm in the acute laminitis or founder case, in my hands it has failed to do any good either. In chronic founder Type 2 cases it is contraindicated by increasing the rate of resorption of the pedal bones.

Of the last group, the anti-clotting drugs, there is really only one which is safe to use in combination with NSAIDs, Heparin. This is available by injection and can be given under the skin or intravenously. In my experience it is of use only in the early stages of the disease, i.e. the first 72 hours.

Nerve blocks

In order to deaden the feet some vets will use nerve blocks. This involves injecting local anaesthetic around the nerves which supply the foot. The nerves are located alongside the arteries at the back and sides of the fetlock joints (see Fig. 9). This was more popular in the days when it was thought that exercise was beneficial to improve the circulation in the feet. Although this treatment certainly removes the pain of laminitis, as with the use of pain killers the danger is that the horse will physically tear apart the laminae by increased weight bearing. Additionally, little is known about how the nerve supply controls the blood vessels in the foot. Blocking the nerves may worsen the constriction of the arteries. *Therefore I would never block a horse's feet if it had laminitis, certainly not if it was foundered or a sinker.*

Exercise

Exercise was always recommended as a treatment for laminitis, the theory being that exercise promoted circulation in the feet. The problem in laminitis and founder is not a lack of circulation, in fact there is a greatly increased amount of blood entering the foot. The problem is that there is greatly reduced *perfusion*, i.e. the blood is entering the foot in greater quantities than normal and then going straight out again via the arteriovenous anastomoses (AV shunts) to the veins without nourishing the tissues of the corium. No amount of exercise is going to improve the perfusion within the foot; this can only be done by relaxing the constriction in the arteries and closing the AV shunts.

Again, the more exercise taken the worse the mechanical strain on the laminae. On humanitarian grounds there is also no justification for making an animal in such pain walk about. The human analogy is to walk on the tip of one finger and toe per limb and have the nail tearing away from the quick as you go. Not a pleasant experience, I am sure.

I recommend absolute box rest, at least until the animal has recovered sufficiently to walk around the stable without pain killers and without lameness. After that I suggest a period of one month walking out in hand two or three times a day for 15 minutes at a time. Alternatively the animal can be turned loose into a quiet arena to amble about at his own pace. Nothing in the way of ridden exercise should be attempted for a month and then the animal should be brought back into work gradually.

Stabling and Bedding

Ideally the animal should be in a stable large enough for it to turn round easily. Turning is usually the most painful movement for lame horses and it certainly is for laminitis cases. The stable should be well insulated to prevent the extremes of temperature which can occur in single thickness wood walled stables. I prefer to use a clean whitewood shaving, with large leaf-like pieces rather than small dusty shavings. Alternatively, paper bedding is acceptable. The lack of dust in the bedding can be particularly important if the animal is down most of the time with his nose in the bed. I use these types of bedding because they can be kept relatively clean and dry and are not eaten by the horses. For horses which are recumbent for much of the day there are important factors in their management, the heat of the stable/bedding (paper tends to be a warmer bed than shavings) and the amount of 'bottom' to the bed. Recumbent horses tend to paddle through a bed and soon end up lying on the concrete. An old bed with a good dry 'bottom' resists this more than a new bed. For these reasons I do not use straw as it is readily eaten, particularly if the animal is on a diet, and it does not form a dry bottom. Deep litter straw bedding is bad for horse's feet because the bed is wet underneath. The chemicals formed in a deep litter or dirty bed can actually attack the horn of the feet. There are also considerable amounts of ammonia produced which is bad for the lungs.

Chapter 5
THE 'CAUSES' OF LAMINITIS

None of the following are really causes, as we do not exactly know what precisely causes an animal to suffer from laminitis. We do know that there is a number of situations which commonly predispose animals to suffer the disease. These predisposing factors I have listed below; they can occur singly or in combination.

1. Obesity/Overeating

This is the group responsible for most of the cases of laminitis and founder seen in the UK. They are all due to managemental errors. It must be remembered that most of the native ponies were bred in regions where the available vegetation is sparse. Bringing such ponies down onto lowland grasses which have been selectively bred for their nutritional value and which are usually chemically fertilized, is to court disaster. In addition, most native ponies are greedy and few are asked to do any work; put these things together and you have a recipe for laminitis. Many horses and ponies first suffer an attack of laminitis or founder when they are away at stud. Mares at stud are managed on a group or herd basis rather than individually. The statement that native ponies cannot tolerate modern grass pastures has been shown to be due to a metabolic difference between ponies and horses. Ponies and cobs use their feed more efficiently, the food being stored as fat for harder times. This metabolic difference is in part due to insulin insensitivity in ponies. The pony's muscle and liver tending to convert the glucose absorbed from the gut to fat rather than use it immediately for energy or store it as glycogen. This innate resistance to the action of insulin is also thought to contribute to vasoconstriction in the feet by encouraging the formation of vasoactive compounds. From what has been discussed so far it can be appreciated that prevention of laminitis is much easier than cure. Allowing ponies free range on cattle pasture is asking for trouble. It is not a question of too much protein or too much carbohydrate, protein will be used as an energy source if there is insufficient carbohydrate in the diet. As a rough rule of thumb native ponies and most horse's can live and perform all but hard work when fed a forage based diet. This means hay and alfalfa, no cereals, no cooling mixes, no herbal mixes, no nuts, just good straightforward forage.

2. Toxaemia

Any animal which suffers toxaemia is predisposed to laminitis and founder. Toxaemia means the circulation of toxins, be they chemical, viral or bacterial, in the blood stream. Such conditions as pleurisy, pneumonia, diarrhoea, retained foetal membranes after foaling are all common causes of equine toxaemia. Peritonitis associated with colic is a common cause of toxaemia. Overeating of rich food whether it be grass or grains can result in a form of toxaemia. When an excess of rich food is consumed, as it is digested, the acidity of the bowel contents increases. Above a certain acidity the normal bacterial population of the bowel are killed and replaced by bacteria which can survive in the changed conditions. The cells of the original bacteria contain toxins which are released when they die and are absorbed through the bowel wall into the horse's circulation. Toxins in the blood stream under certain conditions and in combination with changes in the animal's hormones can lead to the closing down of the blood flow within the laminar corium which has been shown to be the first change of laminitis.

Mares with a uterine infection at or soon after foaling often founder and founder badly. This is usually associated with a retained placenta (cleansing). Very often the bulk of the cleansing comes away but a small piece from within the tip of the empty horn remains attached and sets up a toxaemia. This is why it is so important to lay out the cleansing from mares after foaling and make sure no bits are missing. If part of the cleansing is retained the mare should receive antibiotic treatment by injection. In addition the uterus should be pumped full of hot water and then siphoned empty repeatedly until the effluent is clear. The offending piece of cleansing can often be removed during this procedure. This uterine lavage should be done twice daily until the infection is overcome.

3. Mechanical/Trauma

In this group are included all conditions which lead to a period of abnormally high or protracted weight bearing. A common scenario would be if a horse was very lame on its right fore leg, for example due to infection or a fracture; it might well founder on the left fore due to the increased weight bearing. It is not just stationary weight bearing which may cause the problem. It is not uncommon for hunters in winter, hammering along the roads, or jumping ponies on the hard summer show grounds to develop laminitis. The mechanism in the latter cases is unlikely to be quite the same as the toxaemia cases. The recurrent trauma may result in direct constriction of the digital vessels or formation of excessive oedema fluid.

4. Bad or irregular foot dressing

The former is the fault of the farrier, the latter the fault of the owner. By bad foot dressing I am particularly referring to chronic founder cases in which it is so important to keep the front walls of the feet rasped back and the heels lowered to the correct height. Failure to do this can lead to recurrent bouts of lameness. The same argument applies to feet if they are neglected for more than 6 weeks. Failure to dress the feet forwards can result in a build up of pressure due to excessive (hyperplastic) laminar horn. Failure to keep the heels at a correct height will allow the phalangeal axis to become broken forward leading to lameness. It is hard work dressing feet forwards and awkward work when dealing with Shetland ponies unless the farrier is a dwarf!

5. Drug related

Some drugs, in particular the corticosteroid group of compounds, are known to cause laminitis, particularly in high risk animals. Corticosteroids have been shown to increase the tendency of the vessels in the foot to constrict, thus cutting down the blood flow. The classic case is the administration of long acting preparations to fat ponies at grass suffering from sweetitch. The corticosteroid will probably give some relief from the irritation of midge bites (the cause of sweetitch) but it might make all the ponies feet founder to the stage of solar prolapse within 48 hours! Sweetitch should be controlled by removing the animal from the midges, stabling at dawn and dusk, and using one of the effective insect killer/repellents which are now available.

High doses of thiabendazole, used to treat the larval stages of red-worms, would occasionally cause animals to founder. This drug is little used these days.

6. Stress

Any form of stress may predispose animals to develop laminitis. The most common would be long journeys, particularly in hot summer or cold winter conditions. When animals are stressed they respond by releasing higher than normal levels of their own corticosteroid hormones from their adrenal glands. This presumably mimics the effects of artificially administered steroid drugs and increases the tendency of the digital vessels to constrict.

7. Pituitary cancer

The pituitary gland is a small but very important gland which is found just under the horse's brain (Fig 47). The pituitary secretes hormones which control all the other endocrine glands in the body and thus the general metabolism. It is unfortunately not uncommon for elderly animals to develop a benign cancer of this gland. The gland starts to enlarge and part of it (the *pars intermedia*) secretes abnormally high doses of hormones which particularly affect the adrenal gland (situated near the kidneys). The animals tend to become Cushingoid; this means they lose condition, drink excessively and may become diabetic. The animals are more prone to secondary infections than normal. If they live long enough all these cases will develop laminitis and founder. The first change seen is a failure to shed their winter coat, the coat then becomes abnormally long or matted (Fig 48 & 49). The animals then tend to sweat more than normal. The change in hair coat may at first be slight and not involving the entire body, for example an Arab developing feather more fitting for a Cob. Many of these cases seem to suffer a severe attack of laminitis in the Autumn. The cancer does not spread and some animals may live into their twenties with such a condition without it making their lives unbearable. Animals under 12 years old are rarely affected. There is at present no effective treatment. Many animals can tolerate the changes in hair

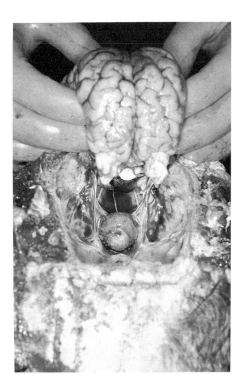

Figure 47. An old pony with a pituitary tumour. The pituitary gland is the spherical tissue in the centre of the picture tucked away beneath the brain. The pituitary gland is abnormally enlarged due to the tumour.

coat and increased thirst up to a point, beyond that the quality of life deteriorates and euthanasia is the best decision. There is a confirmatory test which can be made, this is called the TRH response test and measures the levels of cortisol before and after an intravenous injection of the thyroid releasing hormone.

Laminitis mythology

Drinking cold water after exercise may cause colic but not laminitis.

Allergies There is no scientific evidence to support the role of allergy as a cause of laminitis.

Pregnancy Pregnant animals can develop laminitis just as easily as barren animals.

Oestrus A few mares have been reported to show laminitis-like symptoms in association with the onset of oestrus (when they come into season).

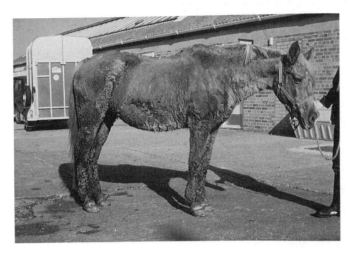

Figure 48. A typical example of the changes in hair coat of a pituitary tumour case.

Figure 49. This pony also has a pituitary tumour, not very hairy but it had been clipped three times already this summer!

Similarly these signs are reported to disappear when the mare finishes her season. These cases are no doubt related to the hormonal status of the mare. However, it should be remembered that these cases are rare and often the mares are high risk animals. They are often overweight and out on good quality pasture.

Heat in the feet Very inconsistent. Foot temperature normally varies throughout the day. Feeling for the temperature of the feet to diagnose laminitis only demonstrates lack of knowledge of the condition.

Standing in streams or cold hosing Any benefit the animal may have felt from the cold immersion was probably more than cancelled by having to walk to get there! Cold water tends to both numb the feet and cause the arteries in the feet to constrict. Pain relief can be effectively achieved by means of drugs and vasoconstriction is the opposite of what is needed in a laminitic foot. Hot water treatments and poulticing have also been tried. Heat will cause beneficial vasodilation; however this dilation is likely to be very weak and short lasting. Much more effective vasodilation can be achieved by phenoxybenzamine.

Bleeding It used to be a popular treatment to make a cut in a jugular vein and remove about a gallon of blood. There was some rationale for this in that this did drop the blood pressure which is abnormally high in laminitis cases. This effect was not long lasting and did weaken the animal albeit temporarily. Drug treatments have now superseded the need for this procedure which was known as jugular phlebotomy.

Laminitis does not just affect the front feet, although the front feet are the more commonly affected. One, two, three or all four feet may be involved, and in any combination.

Chapter 6
FEEDING AND MANAGEMENT

Predisposition to laminitis

In the UK there is no evidence to show that any breed, type or strain of animal is prone to laminitis, assuming sensible management. Some people say that some strains of Welsh pony are prone to laminitis, I doubt this. What is more likely is the ownership of these animals has been in the same family or another member of the showing brigade. The human predisposition for hereditary bad management is certainly proven. What can be said, is that a fat animal is more likely to develop laminitis following challenge with excess food than a lean or fit animal. If an animal is suffering any of the conditions listed in Chapter 5 then it is has a greater than normal risk of developing laminitis, i.e. it is a high risk animal.

Prevention

One of the most important attributes of a skilled horsemaster is to be able to keep the animal at the correct weight. I like to be able to feel a horse's ribs easily and yet not be able to see them. In addition the animal should not have a thick, hard cresty neck. This crest is fat. Another place where mares tend to accumulate fat is in front of the udder. Geldings develop an abnormally thick and pendulous sheath due to the laying down of fat under the skin. More than once have I been called to see an animal which has suddenly developed a swelling, only to find it is a fat depot which the owner has only just noticed! Some animals have a cresty neck without a very obese body, nevertheless the crest can be reduced in size by a rigid diet without emaciating the animal. Some of these animals have abnormal thyroid function. Your veterinary surgeon can test whether your horse's thyroid glands are working normally by taking blood samples before and after injecting a thyroid releasing hormone. Treatment for weak thyroid gland function is available by either supplementing the diet with iodine or by providing synthetic thyroid hormones as tablets or powder.

It requires good management to keep a horse's weight approximately the same the year round. The owner, whilst in daily contact with the animals, cannot always appreciate their gradual change in shape! Be guided by someone who sees the horse only intermittently; the farrier is probably best placed. To be a little more scientific about weight watching it is helpful if a girth measurement is made with a tape measure every time the farrier attends the horse. These measurements should be written down somewhere where they will not be lost, even if it is on the wall of the shoeing box.

I cannot recommend the use of probiotics nor clay preparations as supplements to either prevent or treat laminitis.

Grazing

It is certainly not easy to manage some native ponies at grass during the growing seasons of Spring and Autumn. This is particularly true if they are the garden ornament variety which do no work at all. The secret is to have the animal at the correct body weight before turn out. The guideline of not being able to see their ribs yet being able to feel them easily is worth remembering. If the animal is in this condition before turn out in the Spring you have a somewhat greater safety margin if he should consume too much grass one day. During the growing season the best way of managing pony grazing is by strip grazing with an electric fence. Most ponies will respect an electric fence although you do come across the odd hooligan who either barges straight through it or rolls underneath it. The latter can be stopped by using the mesh type of electric fence while the barger may be deterred by using a higher pulse voltage. If this is not feasible the other way to restrict a pony's grazing is to fit a muzzle for most of the time at grass. There should be a grid in the bottom of the muzzle to enable the pony to drink and nibble whatever grass he can reach. The muzzle should either be fitted by clipping onto the nose band rings of a head collar or by weaving the poll strap of the muzzle through the cheek piece rings in the head collar. A word of warning, make sure there is nothing in the field the pony is likely to get hung up on. Taps on old baths used as water troughs are particularly dangerous. I have seen two horses die after getting hooked up on taps and fracture their necks or drown.

A sensible precaution is to get most of the grass on a new field eaten off by cattle and sheep before turning ponies out. When horses and ponies are grazed for long periods on bald pastures, particular attention must be given to regular worming and dropping picking. Although time consuming, alternate daily gathering of droppings will really help to reduce pasture contamination with worm eggs. *Heavily contaminated or horse sick pastures can produce a sufficiently massive worm challenge to kill young or susceptible individuals. No amount of wormer will save the animal in this situation.*

There seems to be a liking for stabling ponies during the day and turning them out at night in the belief that they will eat less at night. I can assure you this is not the case. By all means graze the pony at night but take the necessary precautions of strip grazing or muzzling just as you should during the day.

There are grass mixtures available which produce a sward of low-nutrient grass which is much safer to feed native ponies.

There is nothing intrinsically dangerous about feeding grass to laminitis or founder cases, I often use haynets full of cut grass at the Clinic as part of the patients' diet. Once people have had an animal suffer an attack of laminitis they tend never to allow it further access to grass. This is usually unnecessary and involves animals being shut up for long periods without exercise; this is not good for them. What makes grass rather dangerous as a feed is;

1. There is rather a lot of it about.
2. Greedy animals can eat great quantities in a relatively short time.
3. The nutritional quality of the grass can change markedly from one fortnight to the next without appearing very different to the naked eye.

Remember there is usually a 'flush' of grass in the Autumn as well as the Spring. I am usually busiest at the Clinic in September and October.

Feeding

There is no great mystery although there is plenty of mythology surrounding the feeding of horses and ponies which have suffered laminitis or founder. The basis of feeding is to feed a high fibre diet low in carbohydrate with sufficient good quality protein, combined with a suitable supplement to ensure all the necessary micronutrients are provided. Unless horses and ponies are in very hard work **they do not need hard feed at all**, they can perform quite satisfactorily on a forage diet. It is certainly sensible to avoid all hard feed ie, cereals, nuts, coarse mixes (whether heating or non-heating), extruded cereal diets etc to any animal that is in a high risk group or has suffered laminitis previously. There seems to be a trend to 'green' the marketing of horse feed, with companies producing meadow mixes, herbal mixes, pasture mixes. These are best avoided if they contain cereals, as most do.

People always ask me how much of this and that they should feed their horse or pony. It is just not possible to say because individual animals' metabolism, their environment and use are so different. This should be borne in mind when following the feeding directions on the outside of bags of horse feed. I use a diet based on the following; a mixture of grass or hay, alfalfa and Farrier's Formula supplement. The grass and hay provide the bulk of the food whilst the alfalfa is used to provide minerals and protein necessary for good horn production. Research at the University of Edinburgh has shown that the minerals in alfalfa are in a protein-bound form which the horse can absorb: this is not always the case with mineral supplements such as limestone or bone flour. Further work has shown that alfalfa fed horses developed better hoof horn quality than horses fed a more traditional English hay diet. Farrier's Formula is the only product which has been independently researched and found to have a normalising effect on the cellular structure and therefore the horn quality of horses with brittle feet. During the same study many of the poor horn quality animals had been receiving biotin for up to two years to little effect. Only 6% of the horses studied were found to have horn defects which responded to biotin supplementation whereas all the horses' feet improved with Farrier's Formula.

Bran is often recommended as an aid to dieting ponies. I never use it. The addition of bran to the diet over a long period is to be avoided as it is high in phosphorous and will result in a feed with too low a calcium:phosphorous ratio. Bran mashes may be used for their laxative properties for 24 hours following an acute overeating episode. This use of bran is acceptable but chronic bran feeding is not recommended. Usually the veterinary surgeon will administer a mixture of liquid paraffin and Epsom salts by stomach tube to help evacuate the bowel and prevent

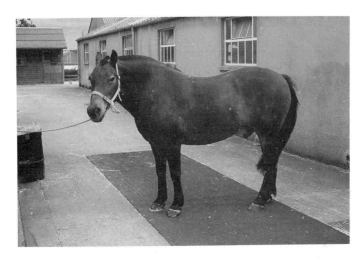

Figure 50. No wonder Tommy got laminitis! Very overweight with a thick crest.

the uptake of bacterial toxins before feeding the bran mashes. I have found a mixture of alfalfa and chopped straw very useful for dieting ponies. This is commercially available from Dengie Crops as Hi Fi (Figs. 50 & 51). A fat Shetland would only need 0.5 kg (about 1.25 lbs) of Hi

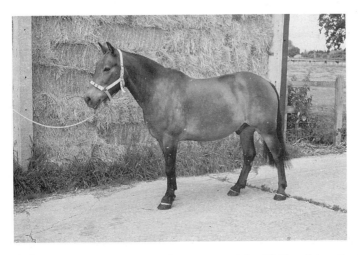

Figure 51. After 3 months on a diet of 3 lbs hay, 2.5 lbs Hi Fi and 6 oz Farrier's Formula daily, Tommy is ready for life in the fast lane.

Fi twice a day with 0.75 kg of hay also twice a day. A handy tip to help keep horses and ponies occupied for longer in the stable when they are on a diet is to spread the hay throughout the bed rather than dump it in one pile or put it in a haynet. It takes them much longer to find and eat the hay. This presupposes excellent stable management. Some animals occupy themselves trying to eat a swede hung from the stable roof.

There are several factors which make the feeding of horses these days more difficult than it need be. One is the pressure from friends to try the latest fad in horse feed. The marketing of horse feed pressurises the horse owner to feed more and more. Another factor is the ridiculous and damaging tendency of most show judges only to award rosettes to animals which are grossly overweight.

A fat 15 hands cob may only need 0.5 kg (1.25 lbs) of Alfa A, 0.5 kg (1.25 lbs) of Hi Fi and 2.5 lbs of hay twice a day, and nothing else but water, if it is to lose weight. It will have to be kept off grass during this period whilst it loses weight. When such a pony has been dieted to a satisfactory bodyweight, access to one to two hours grass daily, in addition to the hay and Hi Fi, is likely to be enough to maintain condition. Fat animals need to be dieted, not starved. Starvation or too drastic a reduction in feed can lead to a condition known as hyperlipaemia. This occurs commonly in fat ponies, particularly fat Shetland ponies and most commonly in fat Shetland ponies in the last third of pregnancy. If the energy value of the diet is suddenly reduced the animal will mobilise fat reserves to provide the missing energy. In cases of hyperlipaemia the mobilisation gets out of control with excessive quantities of liquid fat being released into the blood stream. Hyperlipaemia is often fatal.

Chapter 7
DIAGNOSIS AND
FIRST AID TREATMENT

How to diagnose laminitis

Any change in normal behavious means the animal is unwell. Owners should become familiar with feeling the strength of pulsation in the digital arteries at the fetlock joint of their animals (Fig 9). Only if you know the normal strength of this pulsation (they do vary a little between individuals) will you know when the pulsation is stronger than normal. A stronger than normal pulse indicates laminitis (or an infection or inflammation in the foot). The chance of a stronger than normal pulse in more than one foot indicating a condition other than laminitis is remote. Also, get used to feeling the normal contours of the coronary bands, only then will you be able to appreciate the depression characteristic of founder. Another useful sign in the early stages of laminitis is resentment of mild pressure on the coronary band above the toe. Most laminitis cases resent tapping or pressure applied to the sole of the foot, between the point of frog and the toe.

Heat in the feet is a most misleading sign of laminitis and should not be used to make a diagnosis. The temperature of the feet has been shown to vary in rhythmic manner during the day in normal horses. This is because as the foot cools, a flush of blood will be sent through the foot to warm it up in a cyclic rhythm. The frequency of this flush is proportional to the environmental temperature. In laminitis, the early change is a reduction in blood supply to the laminae, at this stage the feet will be cooler than normal. Little significance should be ascribed to an apparent increase in foot temperature, unless the feet are very hot to the touch over a period of hours.

Remember that the severity of laminitis can vary tremendously. Some cases show a mild lameness, noticeable at trot, of one leg, whereas others are noticed first with the horse down, sweating and blowing like a colic or azoturia case. Laminitis, founder and sinker cases are reluctant to move. Laminitis and founder cases tend to walk on their heels, this is because their toes are relatively more painful. Sinker cases, if they can walk at all, may well walk flat footed and slap their feet down, a similar gait to a wobbler.

What to do if your animal seems to have laminitis

Firstly call a vet who routinely deals with horses. If the animal is at pasture, bring it into a stable, well bedded with clean shavings or paper. If the animal will not even walk a few steps you will have to wait for your vet to arrive before you can move it. If the horse is very lame and the stable is some distance away it will be better to travel it in a low loading trailer rather than make the horse walk. Do not let it eat any more grass in the meantime. If it is not possible to trailer the animal to the stable frog supports should be fitted before it starts to walk. Do not remove the horse's shoes at this stage.

When the animal has reached the stable, a decision has to be made whether to remove the shoes or not. As a general rule, I would remove the shoes from an animal with a concave sole and enough wall to keep the sole of the foot off the ground. If the sole of the foot is flat or there is insufficient wall I would leave the shoes on. Fit frog supports at this stage; obviously thicker frog supports will have to be used on the shod animal to allow for the thickness of the shoe. The only other situation in which I would remove the shoes is if the foot is grossly overgrown and imbalanced or it has been badly shod giving little or no cover and support to the heels.

Chapter 8

PROGNOSIS

What factors affect the prognosis

A study was carried out at the Laminitis Clinic to try and find out which factors were important in determining the outcome of a case of laminitis, founder or sinking. All the animals which were referred to the Clinic were allocated to one of four **Groups** on admission. They were ascribed to these Groups just by clinical examination, ie, without the use of special techniques like blood samples or X-rays. The animals were described as (1) Laminitic (2) Acutely Foundered (3) Sinkers or (4) Chronic Founder cases. Some cases were put down without treatment being attempted because they were either too severely lame or the owners were not prepared or able to cope with their management. The remainder were all treated at the Clinic and then after a period of at least 6 months their progress was recorded and they were **categorised** accordingly. Category 1 cases were either dead or unrideable and Category 2 cases were back doing their normal work, rideable and sound without any painkillers. The following Table shows how the animals were grouped and categorised.

Results of treatment in Categories and Groups

Group	Totals		Sinkers		Acute Founder		Laminitic		Chronic Founder	
Totals	**140**		**13**	(9%)	**49**	(35%)	**18**	(13%)	**60**	(43%)
Category 1 (Dead/ Unrideable)	**40**	(29%)	**12**	(9%)	**9**	(6%)	**1**	(1%)	**18**	(13%)
Category 2 (Alive & Sound)	**100**	(71%)	**1**	(1%)	**40**	(29%)	**17**	(12%)	**42**	(30%)

Percentage figures are in relation to the total of 140 animals (recorded to the largest integer).

In order to discover which factors were the most useful in determining the outcome of the case, information regarding both the animal's physical characteristics and measurements taken from X-rays of the feet were gathered. Horse height, Number of feet involved, Size of foot, Presence of solar prolapse, Angle S (Figs. 52–54), Angle T, Angle U, Angle H, Angle R, Wall thickness WT, Founder distance D, Category and finally the Group to which the animal had been ascribed on admission were recorded. The 'worst' or most abnormal value was taken for each animal (thus allowing for the fact that not all feet were similarly affected). These data were entered into a computer which was then programmed to select the most valuable prognostic parameters. Of all these parameters the computer chose the **Group** as the most useful thing to know about a case in order to predict outcome. This means that each of the Groups carries a statistically significantly different prognosis. If you did not tell the computer in which Group the animal had been placed, the next most useful thing to know was founder distance D.

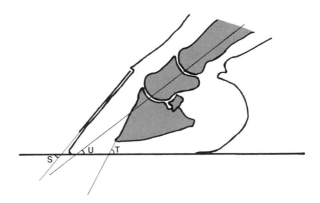

Figure 52. This diagram shows how the three angles S, U and T were measured from X-rays of the feet when the horse was first presented at the Clinic. From these angles two more H and R were calculated;

Angle T minus Angle S = Angle H

Angle T minus Angle U = Angle R

When people say an animal has x degrees of pedal bone rotation they usually mean he has an Angle H of x degrees.

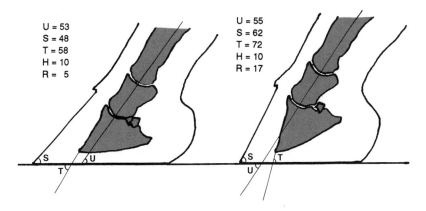

Figure 53. To illustrate how meaningless consideration of one angle is in terms of describing and making prognostic statements about laminitis cases consider the above figure. The angles in the two diagrams are listed beside them. I have purposely drawn them so that Angle H is the same in both; 10 degrees. I think you will see that in the figure on the left the phalangeal axis is straight whereas on the right there is true pedal bone rotation in relation both to the proximal phalanges and to the ground. This is reflected by different Angle R's. Assuming these were acute or old founder cases the one on the left may only need a foot dressing whilst that on the right may need the deep flexor tendon cutting; very different treatments and prognoses for the same angle of rotation!

Therefore, it is important to be able to recognise which of the four groups your animal fits into in order to evaluate its chances of recovering. This presupposes that the animals were all treated according to the same principles as we use at the Laminitis Clinic. Other treatments may give different results. The treatment regime of the Clinic is the only one for which the results of treatment have been published. The next most important thing to examine having found out which group the animal belongs to is to X-ray its feet using the technique described earlier. This will allow accurate measurement of the founder distance. Although at present it is not possible to say that beyond a certain founder distance the horse will definitely not become sound again, it is possible to give a percentage probability. For instance with a founder distance of 15 mm

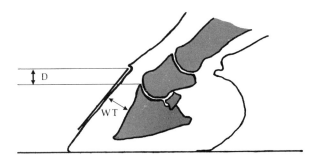

Figure 54. In addition to the three angles S, U and T; two distances were also measured from the X-rays of each foot on admission to the Laminitis Clinic. **WT** or wall thickness is the distance from the wire marker sellotaped to the front of the hoof wall to the front surface of the pedal bone. The distance being measured half way up the front and at right angles to the front surface of the pedal bone. **D** the founder distance was the vertical distance between the top of the wire (placed where the horn changes from hard to soft) and the top of the extensor process.

the horse has about a 37% chance of returning to soundness after treatment (Fig 55).

The factors which have been used to decide on prognosis in the past are uncontrollable pain, presence of solar prolapse, and an angle of rotation, Angle H, greater than 11.5 degrees. Certainly the first factor must be considered on humane grounds; in my experience there are few animals which cannot be made relatively comfortable by drug and foot treatments. The presence of solar prolapse was shown to be unrelated to outcome, in the Clinic study. There were more horses showing solar prolapse which fully recovered than those which died (Figs 56 & 57). The measurement of Angle H (often referred to as an angle of rotation) was shown to be unrelated to outcome, in other words one may as well measure the length of the horse's ears as measure Angle H if you want to predict outcome.

There are several general factors which may indirectly affect the prognosis. Large, flat, wide feet tend to be inherently weaker structures than

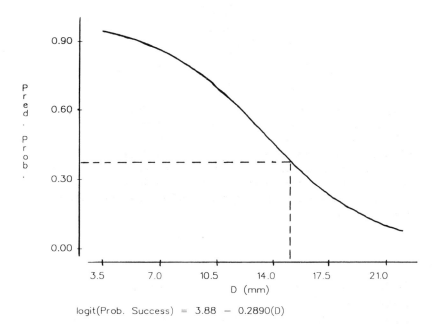

logit(Prob. Success) = 3.88 − 0.2890(D)

Figure 55. From the data entered during the study on prognostic indicators the computer was able to draw a graph indicating the probability of an acute founder or sinker case recovering for a given founder distance D. Although the conclusions which can be drawn from this graph should not be regarded as being cast in tablets of stone, the recognition of Group, and measurement of founder distance D represents a more scientific basis on which to make decisions on the life or death of foundered horses.

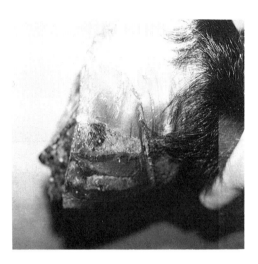

Figure 56. This cob stallion suffered solar prolapse on both front feet. The piece of horny frog and sole covering the tip of the pedal bone protruded 35 mm (1.25 inches) through the horny sole. Measured from the point of the prolapsed tissue to the bottom of the hoof wall at the toe quarters. The founder distance D was only 13.5 mm, the discrepancy being due to gross swelling of the solar corium.

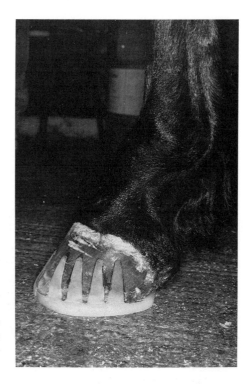

Figure 57. The same foot as shown in Figure 56 six months later. Following careful management, use of Eustace shoes and bilateral deep flexor tenotomies this horse is now sound.

narrower more upright pony type feet. I would far rather deal with a pony type foot than a Thoroughbred foot. Wide, flat feet seem to have a 'narrower safety margin' following founder before they become beyond help. I feel that this is why foundered draught horses have such a bad survival rate. It is not necessarily the great weight of these animals which worsens the prognosis but the shape of their feet.

I regard attention to prognosis as important. By making use of the grouping system and by measuring founder distance it is possible to prevent unnecessary suffering of cases which have such a very slim chance of recovery. Similarly it is now possible to prevent the unnecessary desruction of animals which are very likely to make a full recovery given the correct treatment and a period of recuperation.